CHSPE Practice!

California High School Proficiency Practice Test Questions

Published by

Blue Butterfly Books™

Copyright © 2013, by *Blue Butterfly Books*™, Sheila M. Hynes. ALL RIGHTS RESERVED. No part of this book may be reproduced or transferred in any form or by any means, graphic, electronic, or mechanical, including photocopying, recording, web distribution, taping, or by any information storage retrieval system, without the written permission of the author.

Notice: *Blue Butterfly Books*™ makes every reasonable effort to obtain from reliable sources accurate, complete, and timely information about the tests covered in this book. Nevertheless, changes can be made in the tests or the administration of the tests at any time and *Blue Butterfly Books* ™ makes no representation or warranty, either expressed or implied as to the accuracy, timeliness, or completeness of the information contained in this book. *Blue Butterfly Books* ™ makes no representations or warranties of any kind, express or implied, about the completeness, accuracy, reliability, suitability or availability with respect to the information contained in this document for any purpose. Any reliance you place on such information is therefore strictly at your own risk.

The author(s) shall not be liable for any loss incurred as a consequence of the use and application, directly or indirectly, of any information presented in this work. Sold with the understanding, the author is not engaged in rendering professional services or advice. If advice or expert assistance is required, the services of a competent professional should be sought.

The company, product and service names used in this book are for identification purposes only. All trademarks and registered trademarks are the property of their respective owners. *Blue Butterfly Books* ™ is not affiliate with any educational institution.

We strongly recommend that students check with exam providers for up-to-date information regarding test content.

Please note that CHSPE is administered by the California Department of Education, which was not involved in the production of, and does not endorse, this product.

We strongly recommend that students check with exam providers for up-to-date information regarding test content.

ISBN-13: 978-0993753763 (Blue Butterfly Books)

ISBN-10: 0993753760

Version 6.5 March 2015

Published by
Blue Butterfly Books
Victoria BC Canada

Printed in the USA

Sustainability and Eco-Responsibility

Here at *Blue Butterfly Books*™, trees are valuable to Mother Earth and the health and wellbeing of everyone. Minimizing our ecological footprint and effect on the environment, we choose Create Space, an eco-responsible printing company.

Electronic routing of our books reduces greenhouse gas emissions, worldwide. When a book order is received, the order is filled at the printing location closest to the client. Using environmentally friendly publishing technology, of the Espresso book printing machine, *Blue Butterfly Books*™ are printed as they are requested, saving thousands of books, and trees over time. This process offers the stable and viable alternative keeping healthy sustainability of our environment.

All paper is acid-free, and interior paper stock is made from 30% post-consumer waste recycled material. Safe for children, Create Space also verifies the materials used in the print process are all CPSIA-compliant.

By purchasing this *Blue Butterfly Books*™, you have supported Full Recovery and Preservation of The Karner Blue Butterfly. Our logo is the Karner Blue Butterfly, Lycaeides melissa samuelis, a rare and beautiful butterfly species whose only flower for propogation is the blue lupin flower. The Karner Butterfly is mostly found in the Great Lakes Region of the U.S.A. Recovery planning is in action, for the return of Karner Blue in Canada led by the National Recovery Strategy. The recovery goals and objectives are aimed at recreating suitable habitats for the butterfly and encourage the growth of blue lupines - the butterfly's natural ideal habitat.

For more info on the Karner Blue Butterfly, feel free to visit:

http://www.albanypinebush.org/conservation/wildlife-management/karner-blue-butterfly-recovery

http://www.wiltonpreserve.org/conservation/karner-blue-butterfly.

Contents

6	**Getting Started**	
	The CHSPE Study Plan	7
	Making a Study Schedule	7
13	**Practice Test Questions Set 1**	
	Answer Key	68
89	**Practice Test Questions Set 2**	
	Answer Key	140
160	**Conclusion**	
161	**CHSPE Test Strategy**	

Getting Started

CONGRATULATIONS! By deciding to take the California High School Proficiency Exam (CHSPE), you have taken the first step toward a great future! Of course, there is no point in taking this important examination unless you intend to do your very best to earn the highest grade you possibly can. That means getting yourself organized and discovering the best approaches, methods and strategies to master the material. Yes, that will require real effort and dedication on your part but if you are willing to focus your energy and devote the study time necessary, before you know it you will be on you way to a brighter future.

We know that taking on a new endeavour can be a little scary, and it is easy to feel unsure of where to begin. That's where we come in. This study guide is designed to help you improve your test-taking skills, show you a few tricks of the trade and increase both your competency and confidence.

The California High School Proficiency Exam

The CHSPE exam is composed of three modules, English Language Arts and Math. The English Language Arts consists of English grammar and usage, vocabulary and an essay. The Math module contains basic High School math.

While we seek to make our guide as comprehensive as possible, note that like all entrance exams, the CHSPE Exam might be adjusted at some future point. New material might be added, or content that is no longer relevant or applicable might be removed. It is always a good idea to give the materials you receive when you register to take the CHSPE a careful review.

The CHSPE Study Plan

Now that you have made the decision to take the CHSPE, it is time to get started. Before you do another thing, you will need to figure out a plan of attack. The very best study tip is to start early! The longer the time period you devote to regular study practice, the likelier that you will retain the material and be able to access it quickly. If you thought that 1x20 is the same as 2x10, guess what? It really is not, when it comes to study time. Reviewing material for just an hour per day over the course of 20 days is far better than studying for two hours a day for only 10 days. The more often you revisit a particular piece of information, the better you will know it. Not only will your grasp and understanding be better, but your ability to reach into your brain and quickly and efficiently pull out the tidbit you need, will be greatly enhanced as well.

The great Chinese scholar and philosopher Confucius believed that true knowledge could be defined as knowing both what you know and what you do not know. The first step in preparing for the CHSPE Exam is to assess your strengths and weaknesses. You may already have an idea of what you know and what you do not know, but evaluating yourself using our Self- Assessment modules for each of the three areas, Math, English and Reading Comprehension, will clarify the details.

Making a Study Schedule

To make your study time most productive you will need to develop a study plan. The purpose of the plan is to organize all the bits of pieces of information in such a way that you will not feel overwhelmed. Rome was not built in a day, and learning everything you will need to know to pass the CHSPE Exam is going to take time, too. Arranging the material you need to learn into manageable chunks is the best way to go. Each study session should make you feel as though you have succeeded in accomplishing your goal, and your goal is simply to learn what you planned to learn during that particular session. Try to organize the content in such a way that each study session builds on previous ones. That way, you will retain the information, be better able to access it, and review the previous bits and pieces at the same time.

Self-assessment

The Best Study Tip! The very best study tip is to start early! The longer you study regularly, the more you will retain and 'learn' the material. Studying for 1 hour per day for 20 days is far better than studying for 2 hours for 10 days.

What don't you know?

The first step is to assess your strengths and weaknesses. You may already have an idea of where your weaknesses are, or you can take our Self-assessment modules for each of the areas, Math, English, Science and Reading Comprehension.

Exam Component	Rate from 1 to 5
English / Language Arts	
Vocabulary	
Grammar & Usage	
Punctuation	
Capitalization	
Essay Writing	
Reading Comprehension	
Math	
Algebra	
Ratio and Probability	
Percent, Decimal, Fractions	
Geometry	

Making a Study Schedule

The key to making a study plan is to divide the material you need to learn into manageable size and learn it, while at the same time reviewing the material that you already know.

Using the table above, any scores of three or below, you need to spend time learning, going over and practicing this subject area. A score of four means you need to review the material, but you don't have to spend time re-learning. A score of five and you are OK with just an occasional review before the exam.

A score of zero or one means you really do need to work on this and you should allocate the most time and give it the highest priority. Some students prefer a 5-day plan and others a 10-day plan. It also depends on how much time you have until the exam.

Here is an example of a 5-day plan based on an example from the table above:

Vocabulary: 1   Study 1 hour everyday – review on last day
Fractions: 3   Study 1 hour for 2 days then ½ hour and then review
Algebra: 4   Review every second day
Grammar & Usage: 2 Study 1 hour on the first day – then ½ hour everyday
Reading Comprehension: 5   Review for ½ hour every other day
Geometry: 5 Review for ½ hour every other day

Using this example, geometry and reading comprehension are good and only need occasional review. Algebra is good and needs 'some' review. Fractions need a bit of work, grammar and usage needs a lot of work and vocabulary is very weak and need most time. Based on this, here is a sample study plan:

Day	Subject	Time
Monday		
Study	Vocabulary	1 hour
Study	Grammar & Usage	1 hour
	½ hour break	
Study	Fractions	1 hour
Review	Algebra	½ hour
Tuesday		
Study	Vocabulary	1 hour
Study	Grammar & Usage	½ hour
	½ hour break	
Study	Fractions	½ hour
Review	Algebra	½ hour
Review	Geometry	½ hour
Wednesday		
Study	Vocabulary	1 hour
Study	Grammar & Usage	½ hour
	½ hour break	
Study	Fractions	½ hour
Review	Geometry	½ hour
Thursday		
Study	Vocabulary	½ hour
Study	Grammar & Usage	½ hour
Review	Fractions	½ hour
	½ hour break	
Review	Geometry	½ hour
Review	Algebra	½ hour
Friday		
Review	Vocabulary	½ hour
Review	Grammar & Usage	½ hour
Review	Fractions	½ hour
	½ hour break	
Review	Algebra	½ hour
Review	Grammar & Usage	½ hour

Using this example, adapt the study plan to your own schedule. This schedule assumes 2 ½ - 3 hours available to study everyday for a 5 day period.

First, write out what you need to study and how much. Next figure out how many days you have before the test. Note, do NOT study on the last day before the test. On the last day before the test, you won't learn anything and will probably only confuse yourself.

Make a table with the days before the test and the number of hours you have available to study each day. We suggest working with 1 hour and ½ hour time slots.

Start filling in the blanks, with the subjects you need to study the most getting the most time and the most regular time slots (i.e. everyday) and the subjects that you know getting the least time (e.g. ½ hour every other day, or every 3rd day).

Tips for making a schedule

Once you make a schedule, stick with it! Make your study sessions reasonable. If you make a study schedule and don't stick with it, you set yourself up for failure. Instead, schedule study sessions that are a bit shorter and set yourself up for success! Make sure your study sessions are do-able. Studying is hard work, but after you pass, you can party and take a break!

Schedule breaks. Breaks are just as important as study time. Work out a rotation of studying and breaks that works for you.

Build up study time. If you find it hard to sit still and study for 1 hour straight through, build up to it. Start with 20 minutes, and then take a break. Once you get used to 20-minute study sessions, increase the time to 30 minutes. Gradually work you way up to 1 hour.

40 minutes to 1 hour are optimal. Studying for longer than this is tiring and not productive. Studying for shorter isn't long enough to be productive.

Studying Math. Studying Math is different from studying other subjects because you use a different part of your brain. The best way to study math is to practice everyday.

This will train your mind to think in a mathematical way. If you miss a day or days, the mathematical mind-set is gone and you have to start all over again to build it up.

Study and practice math everyday for at least 5 days before the exam.

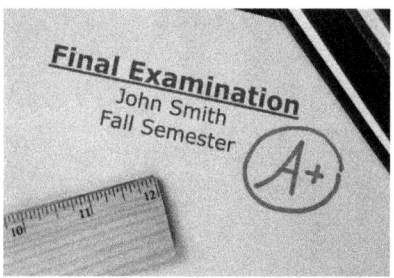

Practice Test Questions Set 1

The questions below are not the same as you will find on the CHSPE - that would be too easy! And nobody knows what the questions will be and they change all the time. Below are general questions that cover the same subject areas as the CHSPE. So, while the format and exact wording of the questions may differ slightly, and change from year to year, if you can answer the questions below, you will have no problem with the CHSPE.

For the best results, take these Practice Test Questions as if it were the real exam. Set aside time when you will not be disturbed, and a location that is quiet and free of distractions. Read the instructions carefully, read each question carefully, and answer to the best of your ability.
Use the bubble answer sheets provided. When you have completed the Practice Questions, check your answer against the Answer Key and read the explanation provided.

Do not attempt more than one set of practice test questions in one day. After completing the first practice test, wait two or three days before attempting the second set of questions.

Reading Answer Sheet

1. Ⓐ Ⓑ Ⓒ Ⓓ
2. Ⓐ Ⓑ Ⓒ Ⓓ
3. Ⓐ Ⓑ Ⓒ Ⓓ
4. Ⓐ Ⓑ Ⓒ Ⓓ
5. Ⓐ Ⓑ Ⓒ Ⓓ
6. Ⓐ Ⓑ Ⓒ Ⓓ
7. Ⓐ Ⓑ Ⓒ Ⓓ
8. Ⓐ Ⓑ Ⓒ Ⓓ
9. Ⓐ Ⓑ Ⓒ Ⓓ
10. Ⓐ Ⓑ Ⓒ Ⓓ
11. Ⓐ Ⓑ Ⓒ Ⓓ
12. Ⓐ Ⓑ Ⓒ Ⓓ
13. Ⓐ Ⓑ Ⓒ Ⓓ
14. Ⓐ Ⓑ Ⓒ Ⓓ
15. Ⓐ Ⓑ Ⓒ Ⓓ
16. Ⓐ Ⓑ Ⓒ Ⓓ
17. Ⓐ Ⓑ Ⓒ Ⓓ
18. Ⓐ Ⓑ Ⓒ Ⓓ
19. Ⓐ Ⓑ Ⓒ Ⓓ
20. Ⓐ Ⓑ Ⓒ Ⓓ
21. Ⓐ Ⓑ Ⓒ Ⓓ
22. Ⓐ Ⓑ Ⓒ Ⓓ
23. Ⓐ Ⓑ Ⓒ Ⓓ
24. Ⓐ Ⓑ Ⓒ Ⓓ
25. Ⓐ Ⓑ Ⓒ Ⓓ
26. Ⓐ Ⓑ Ⓒ Ⓓ
27. Ⓐ Ⓑ Ⓒ Ⓓ
28. Ⓐ Ⓑ Ⓒ Ⓓ
29. Ⓐ Ⓑ Ⓒ Ⓓ
30. Ⓐ Ⓑ Ⓒ Ⓓ
31. Ⓐ Ⓑ Ⓒ Ⓓ
32. Ⓐ Ⓑ Ⓒ Ⓓ
33. Ⓐ Ⓑ Ⓒ Ⓓ
34. Ⓐ Ⓑ Ⓒ Ⓓ
35. Ⓐ Ⓑ Ⓒ Ⓓ
36. Ⓐ Ⓑ Ⓒ Ⓓ
37. Ⓐ Ⓑ Ⓒ Ⓓ
38. Ⓐ Ⓑ Ⓒ Ⓓ
39. Ⓐ Ⓑ Ⓒ Ⓓ
40. Ⓐ Ⓑ Ⓒ Ⓓ
41. Ⓐ Ⓑ Ⓒ Ⓓ
42. Ⓐ Ⓑ Ⓒ Ⓓ
43. Ⓐ Ⓑ Ⓒ Ⓓ
44. Ⓐ Ⓑ Ⓒ Ⓓ
45. Ⓐ Ⓑ Ⓒ Ⓓ
46. Ⓐ Ⓑ Ⓒ Ⓓ
47. Ⓐ Ⓑ Ⓒ Ⓓ
48. Ⓐ Ⓑ Ⓒ Ⓓ
49. Ⓐ Ⓑ Ⓒ Ⓓ
50. Ⓐ Ⓑ Ⓒ Ⓓ

Language Arts Answer Sheet

1. A B C D
2. A B C D
3. A B C D
4. A B C D
5. A B C D
6. A B C D
7. A B C D
8. A B C D
9. A B C D
10. A B C D
11. A B C D
12. A B C D
13. A B C D
14. A B C D
15. A B C D
16. A B C D
17. A B C D
18. A B C D
19. A B C D
20. A B C D
21. A B C D
22. A B C D
23. A B C D
24. A B C D
25. A B C D
26. A B C D
27. A B C D
28. A B C D
29. A B C D
30. A B C D
31. A B C D
32. A B C D
33. A B C D
34. A B C D
35. A B C D
36. A B C D
37. A B C D
38. A B C D
39. A B C D
40. A B C D
41. A B C D
42. A B C D
43. A B C D
44. A B C D
45. A B C D
46. A B C D
47. A B C D
48. A B C D
49. A B C D
50. A B C D

Mathematics Answer Sheet

1. A B C D
2. A B C D
3. A B C D
4. A B C D
5. A B C D
6. A B C D
7. A B C D
8. A B C D
9. A B C D
10. A B C D
11. A B C D
12. A B C D
13. A B C D
14. A B C D
15. A B C D
16. A B C D
17. A B C D
18. A B C D
19. A B C D
20. A B C D
21. A B C D
22. A B C D
23. A B C D
24. A B C D
25. A B C D
26. A B C D
27. A B C D
28. A B C D
29. A B C D
30. A B C D
31. A B C D
32. A B C D
33. A B C D
34. A B C D
35. A B C D
36. A B C D
37. A B C D
38. A B C D
39. A B C D
40. A B C D
41. A B C D
42. A B C D
43. A B C D
44. A B C D
45. A B C D
46. A B C D
47. A B C D
48. A B C D
49. A B C D
50. A B C D

Reading and Language Arts

Questions 1 – 4 refer to the following passage.

Infectious Diseases

An infectious disease is a clinically evident illness resulting from the presence of pathogenic agents, such as viruses, bacteria, fungi, protozoa, multi-cellular parasites, and unusual proteins known as prions. Infectious pathologies are also called communicable diseases or transmissible diseases, due to their potential of transmission from one person or species to another by a replicating agent (as opposed to a toxin).

Transmission of an infectious disease can occur in many different ways. Physical contact, liquids, food, body fluids, contaminated objects, and airborne inhalation can all transmit infecting agents.

Transmissible diseases that occur through contact with an ill person, or objects touched by them, are especially infective, and are sometimes called contagious diseases. Communicable diseases that require a more specialized route of infection, such as through blood or needle transmission, or sexual transmission, are usually not regarded as contagious.

The term infectivity describes the ability of an organism to enter, survive and multiply in the host, while the infectiousness of a disease shows the comparative ease with which the disease is transmitted. An infection however, is not synonymous with an infectious disease, as an infection may not cause important clinical symptoms. [3]

1. What can we infer from the first paragraph in this passage?

    a. Sickness from a toxin can be easily transmitted from one person to another.

    b. Sickness from an infectious disease can be easily transmitted from one person to another.

    c. Few sicknesses are transmitted from one person to another.

    d. Infectious diseases are easily treated.

2. What are two other names for infections' pathologies?

    a. Communicable diseases or transmissible diseases

    b. Communicable diseases or terminal diseases

    c. Transmissible diseases or preventable diseases

    d. Communicative diseases or unstable diseases

3. What does infectivity describe?

    a. The inability of an organism to multiply in the host

    b. The inability of an organism to reproduce

    c. The ability of an organism to enter, survive and multiply in the host

    d. The ability of an organism to reproduce in the host

4. How do we know an infection is not synonymous with an infectious disease?

    a. Because an infectious disease destroys infections with enough time.

    b. Because an infection may not cause clinical symptoms or impair host function.

    c. We do not. The two are synonymous.

    d. Because an infection is too fatal to be an infectious disease.

Questions 5 – 7 refer to the following passage.

Thunderstorms

The first stage of a thunderstorm is the cumulus stage, or developing stage. In this stage, masses of moisture are lifted upwards into the atmosphere. The trigger for this lift can be insulation heating the ground producing thermals, areas where two winds converge, forcing air upwards, or, where winds blow over terrain of increasing elevation. Moisture in the air rapidly cools into liquid drops of water, which appears as cumulus clouds.

As the water vapor condenses into liquid, latent heat is released which warms the air, causing it to become less dense than the surrounding dry air. The warm air rises in an updraft through the process of convection (hence the term convective precipitation). This creates a low-pressure zone beneath the forming thunderstorm. In a typical thunderstorm, approximately 5×10^8 kg of water vapor is lifted, and the amount of energy released when this condenses is about equal to the energy used by a city of 100,000 in a month. [4]

5. The cumulus stage of a thunderstorm is the

    a. The last stage of the storm

    b. The middle stage of the storm formation

    c. The beginning of the thunderstorm

    d. The period after the thunderstorm has ended

6. One of the ways the air is warmed is

    a. Air moving downwards, which creates a high-pressure zone

    b. Air cooling and becoming less dense, causing it to rise

    c. Moisture moving downward toward the earth

    d. Heat created by water vapor condensing into liquid

7. Identify the correct sequence of events.

   a. Warm air rises, water droplets condense, creating more heat, and the air rises farther.

   b. Warm air rises and cools, water droplets condense, causing low pressure.

   c. Warm air rises and collects water vapor, the water vapor condenses as the air rises, which creates heat, and causes the air to rise farther.

   d. None of the above.

Questions 8 – 10 refer to the following passage.

The US Weather Service

The United States National Weather Service classifies thunderstorms as severe when they reach a predetermined level. Usually, this means the storm is strong enough to inflict wind or hail damage. In most of the United States, a storm is considered severe if winds reach over 50 knots (58 mph or 93 km/h), hail is ¾ inch (2 cm) diameter or larger, or if meteorologists report funnel clouds or tornadoes. In the Central Region of the United States National Weather Service, the hail threshold for a severe thunderstorm is 1 inch (2.5 cm) in diameter. Though a funnel cloud or tornado indicates the presence of a severe thunderstorm, the various meteorological agencies would issue a tornado warning rather than a severe thunderstorm warning.

Meteorologists in Canada define a severe thunderstorm as either having tornadoes, wind gusts of 90 km/h or greater, hail 2 centimeters in diameter or greater, rainfall more than 50 millimeters in 1 hour, or 75 millimeters in 3 hours.

Severe thunderstorms can develop from any type of thunderstorm. [5]

8. What is the purpose of this passage?

a. Explaining when a thunderstorm turns into a tornado

b. Explaining who issues storm warnings, and when these warnings should be issued

c. Explaining when meteorologists consider a thunderstorm severe

d. None of the above

9. It is possible to infer from this passage that

a. Different areas and countries have different criteria for determining a severe storm

b. Thunderstorms can include lightning and tornadoes, as well as violent winds and large hail

c. If someone spots both a thunderstorm and a tornado, meteorological agencies will immediately issue a severe storm warning

d. Canada has a much different alert system for severe storms, with criteria that are far less

10. What would the Central Region of the United States National Weather Service do if hail was 2.7 cm in diameter?

a. Not issue a severe thunderstorm warning.

b. Issue a tornado warning.

c. Issue a severe thunderstorm warning.

d. Sleet must also accompany the hail before the Weather Service will issue a storm warning.

Contents

> Science Self-assessment 81
> Answer Key 91
> Science Tutorials 96
> Scientific Method 96
> Biology 99
> Heredity: Genes and Mutation 104
> Classification 108
> Ecology 110
> Chemistry 112
> Energy: Kinetic and Mechanical 126
> Energy: Work and Power 130
> Force: Newton's Three Laws 132

11. Consider the table of contents above. What page would you find information about natural selection and adaptation?

   a. 81
   b. 90
   c. 110
   d. 132

Questions 12 – 14 refer to the following passage.

Clouds

A cloud is a visible mass of droplets or frozen crystals floating in the atmosphere above the surface of the Earth or other planetary bodies. Another type of cloud is a mass of material in space, attracted by gravity, called interstellar clouds and nebulae. The branch of meteorology which studies clouds is called nephrology. When we are speaking of Earth clouds, water vapor is usually the condensing substance, which forms small droplets or ice crystal. These crystals are typically 0.01 mm in diameter. Dense, deep clouds reflect most light, so they appear white, at least from the top. Cloud droplets scatter light very efficiently, so the farther into a cloud light travels, the weaker it gets. This accounts for the gray or dark appearance at the base of large clouds. Thin clouds may appear to have acquired the color of their environment or background. [6]

12. What are clouds made of?

    a. Water droplets.

    b. Ice crystals.

    c. Ice crystals and water droplets.

    d. Clouds on Earth are made of ice crystals and water droplets.

13. The main idea of this passage is

    a. Condensation occurs in clouds, having an intense effect on the weather on the surface of the earth.

    b. Atmospheric gases are responsible for the gray color of clouds just before a severe storm happens.

    c. A cloud is a visible mass of droplets or frozen crystals floating in the atmosphere above the surface of the Earth or other planetary body.

    d. Clouds reflect light in varying amounts and degrees, depending on the size and concentration of the water droplets.

14. Why are clouds white on top and grey on the bottom?

    a. Because water droplets inside the cloud do not reflect light, it appears white, and the farther into the cloud the light travels, the less light is reflected making the bottom appear dark.

    b. Because water droplets outside the cloud reflect light, it appears dark, and the farther into the cloud the light travels, the more light is reflected making the bottom appear white.

    c. Because water droplets inside the cloud reflects light, making it appear white, and the farther into the cloud the light travels, the more light is reflected making the bottom appear dark.

    d. None of the above.

Questions 15 - 18 refer to the following recipe.

Chocolate Chip Cookies

3/4 cup sugar
3/4 cup packed brown sugar
1 cup butter, softened
2 large eggs, beaten
1 teaspoon vanilla extract
2 1/4 cups all-purpose flour
1 teaspoon baking soda
3/4 teaspoon salt
2 cups semisweet chocolate chips
If desired, 1 cup chopped pecans, or chopped walnuts.
Preheat oven to 375 degrees.

Mix sugar, brown sugar, butter, vanilla and eggs in a large bowl. Stir in flour, baking soda, and salt. The dough will be very stiff.

Stir in chocolate chips by hand with a sturdy wooden spoon. Add the pecans, or other nuts, if desired. Stir until the chocolate chips and nuts are evenly dispersed.

Drop dough by rounded tablespoonfuls 2 inches apart onto a cookie sheet.

Bake 8 to 10 minutes or until light brown. Cookies may look underdone, but they will finish cooking after you take them out of the oven.

15. What is the correct order for adding these ingredients?

      a. Brown sugar, baking soda, chocolate chips
      b. Baking soda, brown sugar, chocolate chips
      c. Chocolate chips, baking soda, brown sugar
      d. Baking soda, chocolate chips, brown sugar

16. What does sturdy mean?

    a. Long
    b. Strong
    c. Short
    d. Wide

17. What does disperse mean?

    a. Scatter
    b. To form a ball
    c. To stir
    d. To beat

18. When can you stop stirring the nuts?

    a. When the cookies are cooked.
    b. When the nuts are evenly distributed.
    c. When the nuts are added.
    d. After the chocolate chips are added.

Questions 19 – 20 refer to the following email.

SUBJECT: MEDICAL STAFF CHANGES

To all staff:

This email is to advise you of a paper on recommended medical staff changes has been posted to the Human Resources website.

The contents are of primary interest to medical staff, other staff may be interested in reading it, particularly those in medical support roles.

The paper deals with several major issues:

    1. Improving our ability to attract top quality staff to the

hospital, and retain our existing staff. These changes will make our position and departmental names internationally recognizable and comparable with North American and North Asian departments and positions.

2. Improving our ability to attract top quality staff by introducing greater flexibility in the departmental structure.

3. General comments on issues to be further discussed in relation to research staff.

The changes outlined in this paper are significant. I encourage you to read the document and send to me any comments you may have, so that it can be enhanced and improved.

Gordon Simms
Administrator,
Seven Oaks Regional Hospital

19. Are all hospital staff required to read the document posted to the Human Resources website?

    a. Yes all staff are required to read the document.

    b. No, reading the document is optional.

    c. Only medical staff are required to read the document.

    d. none of the above are correct.

20. Have the changes to medical staff been made?

    a. Yes, the changes have been made.

    b. No, the changes are only being discussed.

    c. Some of the changes have been made.

    d. None of the choices are correct.

Questions 21 – 25 refer to the following passage.

Navy Seals

The United States Navy's Sea, Air and Land Teams, commonly known as Navy SEALs, are the U.S. Navy's principle special operations force, and a part of the Naval Special Warfare Command (NSWC) as well as the maritime component of the United States Special Operations Command (USSOCOM).

The unit's acronym ("SEAL") comes from their capacity to operate at sea, in the air, and on land – but it is their ability to work underwater that separates SEALs from most other military units in the world. Navy SEALs are trained and have been deployed in a wide variety of missions, including direct action and special reconnaissance operations, unconventional warfare, foreign internal defence, hostage rescue, counter-terrorism and other missions. All SEALs are members of either the United States Navy or the United States Coast Guard.

In the early morning of May 2, 2011 local time, a team of 40 CIA-led Navy SEALs completed an operation to kill Osama bin Laden in Abbottabad, Pakistan about 35 miles (56 km) from Islamabad, the country's capital. The Navy SEALs were part of the Naval Special Warfare Development Group, previously called "Team 6." President Barack Obama later confirmed the death of bin Laden. The unprecedented media coverage raised the public profile of the SEAL community, particularly the counter-terrorism specialists commonly known as SEAL Team 6. [7]

21. Are Navy SEALs part of USSOCOM?

    a. Yes
    b. No
    c. Only for special operations
    d. No, they are part of the US Navy

22. What separates Navy SEALs from other military units?

    a. Belonging to NSWC

    b. Direct action and special reconnaissance operations

    c. Working underwater

    d. Working for other military units in the world

23. What other military organizations do SEALs belong to?

    a. The US Navy

    b. The Coast Guard

    c. The US Army

    d. The Navy and the Coast Guard

24. What other organization participated in the Bin Laden raid?

    a. The CIA

    b. The US Military

    c. Counter-terrorism specialists

    d. None of the above

25. What is the new name for Team 6?

    a. They were always called Team 6

    b. The counter-terrorism specialists

    c. The Naval Special Warfare Development Group

    d. None of the above

Questions 26 – 28 refer to the following passage.

How to Get a Good Nights Sleep

Sleep is just as essential for healthy living as water, air and food. Sleep allows the body to rest and replenish depleted energy levels. Sometimes we may for various reasons experience difficulty sleeping which has a serious effect on our health. Those who have prolonged sleeping problems are facing a serious medical condition and should see a qualified doctor when possible for help. Here is simple guide that can help you sleep better at night.

Try to create a natural pattern of waking up and sleeping around the same time everyday. This means avoiding going to bed too early and oversleeping past your usual wake up time. Going to bed and getting up at radically different times everyday confuses your body clock. Try to establish a natural rhythm as much as you can.

Exercises and a bit of physical activity can help you sleep better at night. If you are having problem sleeping, try to be as active as you can during the day. If you are tired from physical activity, falling asleep is a natural and easy process for your body. If you remain inactive during the day, you will find it harder to sleep properly at night. Try walking, jogging, swimming or simple stretches as you get close to your bed time.

Afternoon naps are great to refresh you during the day, but they may also keep you awake at night. If you feel sleepy during the day, get up, take a walk and get busy to keep from sleeping. Stretching is a good way to increase blood flow to the brain and keep you alert so that you don't sleep during the day. This will help you sleep better night.

A warm bath or a glass of milk in the evening can help your body relax and prepare for sleep. A cold bath will wake you up and keep you up for several hours. Also avoid eating too late before bed.

26. How would you describe this sentence?

    a. A recommendation

    b. An opinion

    c. A fact

    d. A diagnosis

27. Which of the following is an alternative title for this article?

    a. Exercise and a good night's sleep

    b. Benefits of a good night's sleep

    c. Tips for a good night's sleep

    d. Lack of sleep is a serious medical condition

28. Which of the following cannot be inferred from this article?

    a. Biking is helpful for getting a good night's sleep

    b. Mental activity is helpful for getting a good night's sleep

    c. Eating bedtime snacks is not recommended

    d. Getting up at the same time is helpful for a good night's sleep

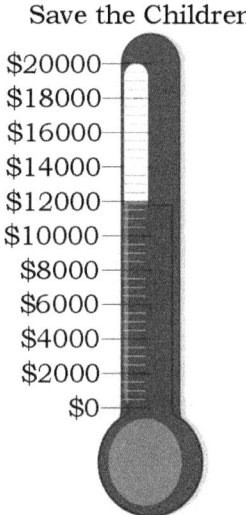

Save the Children

29. Consider the graphic above. The Save the Children fund has a fund-raising goal of $20,000. About how much of their goal have they achieved?

    a. 3/5
    b. 3/4
    c. 1/2
    d. 1/3

30. Consider the graphic above. The Save the Children fund has a fund-raising goal of $16,000. About how much of their goal have they achieved?

    a. 3/5
    b. 3/4
    c. 1/2
    d. 1/3

31. Choose a verb that means fearless or invulnerable to intimidation and fear.

    a. Feeble
    b. Strongest
    c. Dauntless
    d. Super

32. Choose a word that means the same as the underlined word.

I see the differences when they are placed side-by-side and juxtaposed.

    a. Compared
    b. Eliminated
    c. Overturned
    d. Exonerated

33. Choose the meaning of regicide.

    a. v. To endow or furnish with requisite ability, character, knowledge and skill
    b. n. killing of a king
    c. adj. Disposed to seize by violence or by unlawful or greedy methods
    d. v. To refresh after labor

34. Choose the best definition of pernicious.

    a. Deadly
    b. Infectious
    c. Common
    d. Rare

35. After she received her influenza vaccination, Nan thought that she was _____ to the common cold.

    a. Immune
    b. Susceptible
    c. Vulnerable
    d. At risk

36. She performed the gymnastics and stretches so well! I have never seen anyone so <u>nimble</u>.

    a. Awkward
    b. Agile
    c. Quick
    d. Taut

37. Are there any more <u>queries</u>? We have already had so many questions today.

    a. Questions
    b. Commands
    c. Obfuscations
    d. Paradoxes

38. Choose a verb that means to remove a leader or high official from position.

    a. Sack
    b. Suspend
    c. Depose
    d. Dropped

39. Choose the best definition of pedestrian.

    a. Rare
    b. Often
    c. Walking or Running
    d. Commonplace

40. Choose the best definition of petulant.

    a. Patient
    b. Childish
    c. Impatient
    d. Mature

41. Paul's rose bushes were being destroyed by Japanese beetles, so he invested in a good _____.

    a. Fungicide
    b. Fertilizer
    c. Sprinkler
    d. Pesticide

42. Choose the best definition of salient.

    a. v. To make light by fermentation, as dough
    b. adj. Not stringent or energetic
    c. adj. negligible
    d. adj. worthy of note or relevant

43. Choose the best definition of sedentary

    a. n. A morbid condition, due to obstructed excretion of bile or characterized by yellowing of the skin
    b. adj. not moving or sitting at a place
    c. v. To wander from place to place
    d. n. Perplexity

44. The last time that the crops failed, the entire nation experienced months of _____.

   a. Famine
   b. Harvest
   c. Plenitude
   d. Disease

45. Choose the best definition of stint.

   a. Thrifty
   b. Annoyed
   c. Dislike
   d. Insult

46. Choose the best definition of precipitate.

   a. To rain
   b. To throw down
   c. To throw up
   d. to snow

47. Choose the verb that means to build up or strengthen in relation to morals or religion.

   a. Sanctify
   b. Amplify
   c. Edify
   d. Wry

48. Choose the noun that means exit or way out.

   a. Door-jamb
   b. Egress
   c. Regress
   d. Furtherance

49. Choose the best definition of the underlined word.

The tide was in this morning but now it is starting to recede.

   a. Go out
   b. Flow
   c. Swell
   d. Come in

50. Choose the word that means private, personal.

   a. Confidential
   b. Hysteric
   c. Simplistic
   d. Promissory

English Grammar, Punctuation, Capitalization and Usage

Directions: Carefully examine the underlined words in the sentences given below. You may see an error in punctuation, grammar, usage or capitalization. Select the correct version of the sentence from the choices given.

1. To make chicken <u>soup; you</u> must first buy a chicken.

    a. To make chicken soup you must first buy a chicken.

    b. To make chicken soup you must first, buy a chicken.

    c. To make chicken soup, you must first buy a chicken.

    d. None of the choices are correct.

2. To travel around <u>the globe you have</u> to drive 25,000 miles.

    a. To travel around the globe, you have to drive 25000 miles.

    b. To travel around the globe, you have to drive, 25000 miles.

    c. None of the choices are correct.

    d. To travel around the globe, you have to drive 25,000 miles.

3. The dog loved chasing <u>bones; but never ate them:</u> it was running that he enjoyed.

    a. The dog loved chasing bones, but never ate them; it was running that he enjoyed.

    b. The dog loved chasing bones; but never ate them, it was running that he enjoyed.

    c. The dog loved chasing bones, but never ate them, it was running that he enjoyed.

    d. None of the choices are correct.

4. He had not paid the <u>rent, therefore,</u> the landlord changed the locks.

    a. None of the choices are correct.

    b. He had not paid the rent; therefore, the landlord changed the locks.

    c. He had not paid the rent, therefore; the landlord changed the locks.

    d. He had not paid the rent therefore, the landlord changed the locks.

5. If <u>he would have known</u> about the forecast, <u>he would have postponed</u> the camping trip.

    a. He would have postponed the camping trip, if he would have known about the forecast.

    b. None of the choices are correct.

    c. If he have known about the forecast, he would have postponed the camping trip.

    d. If he had known about the forecast, he would have postponed the camping trip.

6. Although you may not see <u>nobody</u> in the dark, it does not mean that <u>nobody</u> is there.

    a. The sentence is correct.

    b. Although you may not see anyone in the dark, it does not mean that not nobody is there.

    c. Although you may not see anyone in the dark, it does not mean that anyone is there.

    d. Although you may not see nobody in the dark, it does not mean that not nobody is there.

7. He <u>don't</u> have any money to buy clothes and neither <u>does</u> I.

    a. He doesn't have any money to buy clothes and neither do I.

    b. He doesn't have any money to buy clothes and neither does I.

    c. He don't have any money to buy clothes and neither do I.

    d. None of the choices are correct.

8. Choose the sentence with the correct grammar.

    a. Because it really don't matter, I don't care if I go there.
    b. Because it really doesn't matter, I doesn't care if I go there.
    c. Because it really doesn't matter, I don't care if I go there.
    d. Because it really don't matter, I don't care if I go there.

9. When we <u>go</u> to the picnic, we will <u>take</u> potato salad and wieners.

    a. None of the choices are correct.

    b. If you come to the picnic, bring potato salad and wieners.

    c. When we go to the picnic, we will bring potato salad and wieners.

    d. If you come to the picnic, take potato salad and wieners.

10. The older children have already eat their dinner, but the baby has not yet ate anything.

   a. The older children have already eat their dinner, but the baby has not yet eaten anything.

   b. The older children have already eaten their dinner, but the baby has not yet ate anything.

   c. The older children have already eaten their dinner, but the baby has not yet eaten anything.

   d. The sentence is correct.

11. Newer cars use less gasoline, and produce less emissions.

   a. Newer cars use fewer gasoline, and produce fewer emissions.

   b. None of the choices are correct.

   c. Newer cars use less gasoline, and produce fewer emissions.

   d. Newer cars fewer less gasoline, and produce less emissions.

12. He should have went to the appointment; instead, he gone to the beach.

   a. He should have went to the appointment; instead, he went to the beach.

   b. He should have gone to the appointment; instead, he went to the beach.

   c. None of the choices are correct.

   d. He should have gone to the appointment; instead, he gone to the beach.

13. However; I believe that he didn't really try that hard.

   a. However, I believe that he didn't really try that hard.

   b. However I believe that he didn't really try that hard.

   c. None of the choices are correct.

   d. However: I believe that he didn't really try that hard.

14. It's important for you to know it's official name; it's called the Confederate Museum.

　　a. Its important for you to know its official name; its called the Confederate Museum.

　　b. None of the choices are correct.

　　c. It's important for you to know its official name; it's called the Confederate Museum.

　　d. Its important for you to know it's official name; it's called the Confederate Museum.

15. Once the chickens had laid their eggs, they laid on their nests to hatch them.

　　a. Once the chickens had layed their eggs, they lay on their nests to hatch them.

　　b. Once the chickens had lay their eggs, they lay on their nests to hatch them.

　　c. Once the chickens had laid their eggs, they lay on their nests to hatch them.

　　d. None of the choices are correct.

16. The mother would not of punished her daughter if she could of avoided it.

　　a. The mother would not of punished her daughter if she could have avoided it.

　　b. The mother would not have punished her daughter if she could of avoided it.

　　c. None of the choices are correct.

　　d. The mother would not have punished her daughter if she could have avoided it.

17. Even with <u>an</u> speed limit sign clearly posted, <u>a</u> inattentive driver may drive too fast.

    a. Even with an speed limit sign clearly posted, an inattentive driver may drive too fast.

    b. Even with a speed limit sign clearly posted, a inattentive driver may drive too fast.

    c. None of the choices are correct.

    d. Even with a speed limit sign clearly posted, an inattentive driver may drive too fast.

18. <u>Accept</u> for the roses, she did not <u>accept</u> John's frequent gifts.

    a. Except for the roses, she did not accept John's frequent gifts.

    b. Accept for the roses, she did not except John's frequent gifts.

    c. None of the choices are correct.

    d. Except for the roses, she did not except John's frequent gifts.

19. Although he continued to <u>advice</u> me, I no longer took his <u>advise</u>.

    a. Although he continued to advise me, I no longer took his advice.

    b. Although he continued to advice me, I no longer took his advise.

    c. Although he continued to advise me, I no longer took his advise.

    d. None of the choices are correct.

20. To <u>adopt</u> to the climate, we had to <u>adopt</u> a different style of clothing.

  a. To adapt to the climate, we had to adapt a different style of clothing.

  b. To adopt to the climate, we had to adopt a different style of clothing.

  c. To adapt to the climate, we had to adopt a different style of clothing.

  d. None of the choices are correct.

21. When he's <u>between</u> friends, Robert seems confident, but, <u>between</u> you and me, he is really shy.

  a. None of the choices are correct.

  b. When he's among friends, Robert seems confident, but, among you and me, he is really shy.

  c. When he's between friends, Robert seems confident, but, among you and me, he is really shy.

  d. When he's among friends, Robert seems confident, but, between you and me, he is really shy.

22. I will be finished <u>at about</u> ten in the morning, and will be arriving at home <u>at</u> 6:30.

  a. I will be finished at ten in the morning, and will be arriving at home at about 6:30.

  b. None of the choices are correct.

  c. I will be finished at about ten in the morning, and will be arriving at home at about 6:30.

  d. I will be finished at ten in the morning, and will be arriving at home at 6:30.

23. Beside the red curtains and pillows, there was a red rug besides the couch.

    a. Beside the red curtains and pillows, there was a red rug beside the couch.

    b. Besides the red curtains and pillows, there was a red rug beside the couch.

    c. Besides the red curtains and pillows, there was a red rug besides the couch.

    d. None of the choices are correct.

24. Although John may swim very well, the lifeguard may not allow him to swim in the pool.

    a. Although John can swim very well, the lifeguard may not allow him to swim in the pool.

    b. None of the choices are correct.

    c. Although John can swim very well, the lifeguard can not allow him to swim in the pool.

    d. Although John may swim very well, the lifeguard may not allow him to swim in the pool.

25. Her continuous absences caused a continuous disruption at the office.

    a. Her continuous absences caused a continual disruption at the office.

    b. Her continual absences caused a continuous disruption at the office.

    c. Her continual absences caused a continual disruption at the office.

    d. None of the choices are correct.

26. During the famine, the Irish people had to <u>immigrate</u> to other countries; many of them <u>immigrated</u> to the United States.

    a. During the famine, the Irish people had to emigrate to other countries; many of them immigrated to the United States.

    b. None of the choices are correct.

    c. During the famine, the Irish people had to emigrate to other countries; many of them emigrated to the United States.

    d. During the famine, the Irish people had to immigrate to other countries; many of them emigrated to the United States.

27. His home was <u>further</u> than we expected; <u>further</u>, the roads were very bad.

    a. His home was farther than we expected; farther, the roads were very bad.

    b. His home was farther than we expected; further, the roads were very bad.

    c. None of the choices are correct.

    d. His home was further than we expected; farther, the roads were very bad.

28. The volunteers brought groceries and toys to the homeless shelter; the latter was given to the staff, while the groceries were given directly to the children.

    a. The volunteers brought groceries and toys to the homeless shelter; the latter were given to the staff, while the former were given directly to the children.

    b. The volunteers brought groceries and toys to the homeless shelter; the former was given to the staff, while the latter was given directly to the children.

    c. The volunteers brought groceries and toys to the homeless shelter; the groceries were given to the staff, while the former was given directly to the children.

    d. None of the choices are correct.

29. You shouldn't <u>sit</u> in that chair wearing black pants; I <u>sit</u> the white cat there just a moment ago.

    a. You shouldn't sit in that chair wearing black pants; I set the white cat there just a moment ago.

    b. You shouldn't set in that chair wearing black pants; I sit the white cat there just a moment ago.

    c. You shouldn't set in that chair wearing black pants; I set the white cat there just a moment ago.

    d. None of the choices are correct.

30. Mars is the god of war.

    a. Mars is the god or war.
    b. Mars is the God of war.
    c. Mars is the God of War.
    d. None of the choices are correct.

31. This is her third term as <u>Mayor of chicago</u>.

    a. This is her third term as mayor of Chicago.
    b. This is her third term as Mayor of Chicago.
    c. This is her third term as mayor of chicago.
    d. None of the above.

32. I was able to speak with Susan Roberts <u>mayor of tampa</u>.

    a. I was able to speak with Susan Roberts, Mayor of Tampa.

    b. I was able to speak with Susan Roberts, mayor of Tampa.

    c. I was able to speak with Susan Roberts, Mayor of tampa.

    d. None of the Above.

.33. I think <u>thanksgiving</u> is the best <u>Fall Holiday</u>.

a. I think thanksgiving is the best fall holiday.
b. I think Thanksgiving is the best Fall holiday.
c. I think Thanksgiving is the best fall holiday.
d. None of the above.

34. **I will be skipping The Fall 2013 semester.**

a. I will be skipping the Fall 2013 Semester.
b. I will be skipping the fall 2013 semester.
c. I will be skipping the Fall 2013 semester.
d. None of the above.

35. **The man was asked to come with <u>her</u> daughter and <u>his</u> test results.**

a. The man was asked to come with his daughter and her test results.
b. The man was asked to come with her daughter and her test results.
c. The man was asked to come with her daughter and our test results.
d. None of the above.

36. **The tables were layed by the students.**

a. The tables were laid by the students.
b. The tables were lay by the students.
c. The tables were lie by the students.
d. None of the choices are correct.

37. Each boy and girl were given a toy.

    a. Each boy and girl were given a toy.

    b. Each boy and girl was given a toy.

    c. A and B are correct.

    d. None of the choices are correct.

38. His measles are getting better.

    a. His measles is getting better.

    b. The sentence is correct.

    c. Both of the choices are correct.

    d. None of the choices are correct.

39. In spite of the bad weather yesterday, he can still attend the party.

    a. The sentence is correct.

    b. In spite of the bad weather yesterday, he could still attend the party.

    c. In spite of the bad weather yesterday, he may still attend the party.

    d. None of the choices are correct.

40. Any girl that fails the test loses her admission.

    a. Any girl that fails the test loses their admission.

    b. Any girl that fails the test loses our admission.

    c. The sentence is correct.

    d. None of the choices are correct.

41. He <u>ought</u> be back by now.

    a. He ought to be back by now.
    b. The sentence is correct.
    c. He ought come back by now.
    d. None of the choices are correct.

42. The man as well as his son <u>have</u> arrived.

    a. The man as well as his son has arrived
    b. The sentence is correct.
    c. None of the choices are correct.

43. Mark and Peter have talked <u>to each other</u>.

    a. The sentence is correct.
    b. Mark and Peter have talked to one another.
    c. None of the choices are correct.

44. Christians believe that their lord <u>have</u> raise.

    a. Christians believe that their lord have raised.
    b. Christians believe that their lord has risen.
    c. The sentence is correct.
    d. None of the choices are correct.

45. Here are the names of people <u>whom</u> you should contact.

    a. The sentence is correct.
    b. Here are the names of people who you should contact
    c. None of the choices are correct.

46. The sad news are delivered this morning.

  a. The sad news were delivered this morning.
  b. The sentence is correct.
  c. The sad news was delivered this morning.
  d. None of the choices are correct.

47. The World Health Organization (WHO) are meeting by January.

  a. The sentence is correct.
  b. The World Health Organization (WHO) is meeting by January.
  c. None of the choices are correct.

48. They shall have to retire when they reach 60 years of age.

  a. They will have to retire when they reach 60 years of age.
  b. The sentence is correct.
  c. None of the choices are correct.

Mathematics

1. Translate the following into an equation:

six times a number plus five.

  a. 6X + 5
  b. 6(X+5)
  c. 5X + 6
  d. (6 * 5) + 5

2. Translate the following into an equation:

three plus a number times 7 equals 42.

    a. $7(3 + X) = 42$
    b. $3(X + 7) = 42$
    c. $3X + 7 = 42$
    d. $(3 + 7)X = 42$

3. Brad has agreed to buy everyone a Coke. Each drink costs $1.89, and there are 5 friends. Estimate Brad's cost.

    a. $7
    b. $8
    c. $10
    d. $12

4. Estimate 215 x 65.

    a. 1,350
    b. 13,500
    c. 103,500
    d. 3,500

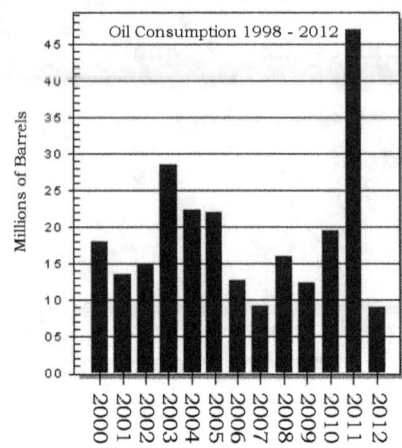

5. The graph above shows oil consumption in millions of barrels for the period, 1998 - 2012. What year did oil consumption peak?

    a. 2011
    b. 2010
    c. 2008
    d. 2009

6. In a certain game, a coin and a dice are rolled, and a player wins if the coin comes up heads, or the dice with a number greater than 4. In 20 games, about how many times will a player win?

    a. 13
    b. 8
    c. 11
    d. 15

7. Sarah weighs 25 pounds more than Tony does. If together they weigh 205 pounds, how much will Sarah weigh approximately in kilograms? Assume 1 pound = 0.4535 kilograms.

    a. 41
    b. 48
    c. 50
    d. 52

8. Choose the expression the figure represents.

    a. $X \leq 1$
    b. $X < 1$
    c. $X > 1$
    d. $X \geq 1$

9. Divide 243 by 3^3

    a. 243
    b. 11
    c. 9
    d. 27

10. What fraction of $1500 is $75?

    a. 1/14
    b. 3/5
    c. 7/10
    d. 1/20

11. Below is the attendance for a class of 45.

Day	Number of Absent Students
Monday	5
Tuesday	9
Wednesday	4
Thursday	10
Friday	6

What is the average attendance for the week?

    a. 88%
    b. 85%
    c. 81%
    d. 77%

12. 2/3 − 2/5 =

    a. 4/10
    b. 1/15
    c. 3/7
    d. 4/15

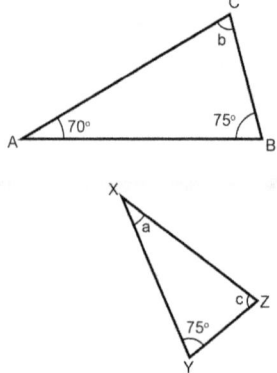

13. What are the respective values of a, b & c if both triangles are similar?

   a. 70°, 70°, 35°
   b. 70°, 35°, 70°
   c. 35°, 35°, 35°
   d. 70°, 75°, 35°

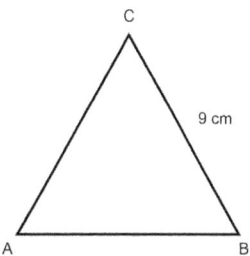

Note: figure not drawn to scale

14. What is the perimeter of the equilateral △ABC above?

   a. 18 cm
   b. 12 cm
   c. 27 cm
   d. 15 cm

15. Express 0.27 + 0.33 as a fraction.

   a. 3/6
   b. 4/7
   c. 3/5
   d. 2/7

16. $7^5 - 3^5 =$

    a. 15,000
    b. 16,564
    c. 15,800
    d. 15,007

17. **What is 2/4 X 3/4 reduced to lowest terms?**

    a. 6/12
    b. 3/8
    c. 6/16
    d. 3/4

18. **Solve the following equation 4(y + 6) = 3y + 30**

    a. y = 20
    b. y = 6
    c. y = 30/7
    d. y = 30

19. **2/3 of 60 + 1/5 of 75 =**

    a. 45
    b. 55
    c. 15
    d. 50

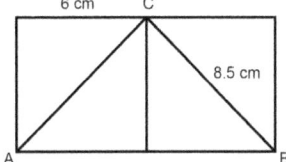

Note: figure not drawn to scale

20. Assuming the 2 quadrangles are identical rectangles, what is perimeter of △ABC in the above shape?

    a. 25.5 cm
    b. 27 cm
    c. 30 cm
    d. 29 cm

21. What is (3.13 + 7.87) X 5?

    a. 65
    b. 50
    c. 45
    d. 55

22. Solve for x if, $10^2 \times 100^2 = 1000^x$

    a. x = 2
    b. x = 3
    c. x = -2
    d. x = 0

23. What is 1/3 of 3/4?

    a. 1/4
    b. 1/3
    c. 2/3
    d. 3/4

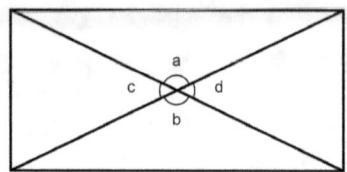

24. What is the sum of all the angles in the rectangle above?

    a. 180°
    b. 360°
    c. 90°
    d. 120°

25. Express 5 x 5 x 5 x 5 x 5 x 5 in exponential form.

    a. 5^6
    b. 10^6
    c. 5^{16}
    d. 5^3

26. Express 9 x 9 x 9 in exponential form and standard form.

    a. 9^3 = 719
    b. 9^3 = 629
    c. 9^3 = 729
    d. 10^3 = 729

27. If y = 4 and x = 3, solve yx^3

    a. -108
    b. 108
    c. 27
    d. 4

28. Divide 0.524 by 10^3

    a. 0.0524
    b. 0.00052
    c. 0.00524
    d. 524

29. If X = 7 solve 3x + 5 – 2x

    a. x = 6
    b. x = 12
    c. x = 1
    d. x = 0

30. (x – 2) / 4 – (3x + 5) / 7 = -3, x=?

    a. 6
    b. 7
    c. 10
    d. 13

31. 2/7 + 2/3 =

    a. 12/23
    b. 5/10
    c. 20/21
    d. 6/21

32. $3^2 \times 3^5$

    a. 3^{17}
    b. 3^5
    c. 4^8
    d. 3^7

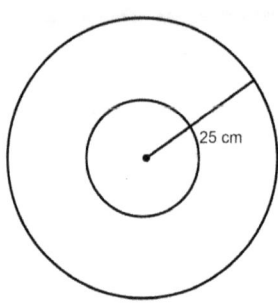

33. What is the distance travelled by the wheel above, if it makes 175 revolutions?

    a. 87.5 π m
    b. 875 π m
    c. 8.75 π m
    d. 8750 π m

34. Expand (x + 7)(x - 3)

    a. $x^2 + 4x - 21$
    b. x + 21
    c. 2x + 4 - 21
    d. 6x - 21 2x + 4x - 21

35. Estimate 2009 x 108.

    a. 110,000
    b. 2,0000
    c. 21,000
    d. 210,000

Note: figure not drawn to scale

36. A tile factory makes custom tiles, shown above, from two types of stone. If a customer requires 200 tiles, how much black stone will be required?

    a. 256 m^2
    b. 2560 m^2
    c. 2.56 m^2
    d. 25.6 m^2

37. Multiply 0.27 by 9^2

    a. 218.7
    b. 21.87
    c. 21
    d. 20.87

38. A woman spent 15% of her income on an item and ends with $120. What percentage of her income is left?

    a. 12%
    b. 85%
    c. 75%
    d. 95%

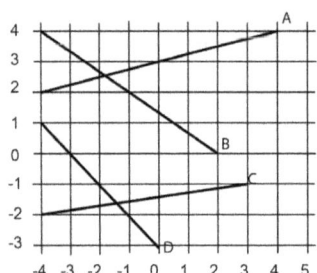

39. Which of the lines above represents the equation 2y − x = 4?

    a. A
    b. B
    c. C
    d. D

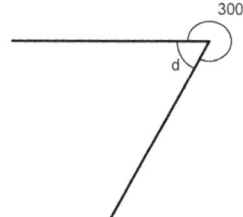

40. What is the measurement of the indicated angle?

    a. 45°
    b. 90°
    c. 60°
    d. 50°

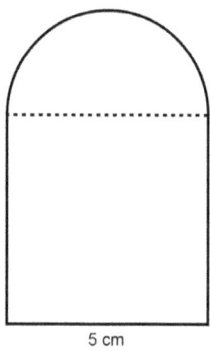

Note: figure not drawn to scale

41. What is the perimeter of the above shape?

    a. 22.85 cm
    b. 20 cm
    c. 15 cm
    d. 25.546 cm

42. Solve $3^8/3^5$

    a. 3^3
    b. 3^5
    c. 3^6
    d. 3^4

43. Solve $3x - 27 = 0$

    a. x = 24
    b. x = 30
    c. x = 9
    d. x = 21

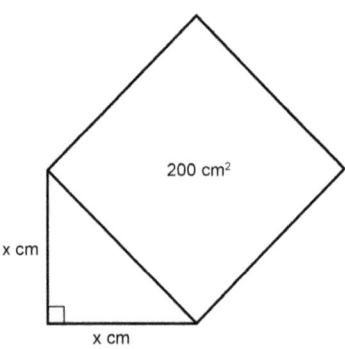

Note: Figure not drawn to scale

44. Assuming the quadrangle in the figure above is square, what is the length of the sides in the triangle above?

    a. 10
    b. 20
    c. 100
    d. 40

45. Solve 3b - 4 + 5b = 0

a. b = 1
b. b = 1/3
c. b = 2
d. b = 1/2

46. 3.14 + 2.73 + 23.7 =

a. 28.57
b. 30.57
c. 29.56
d. 29.57

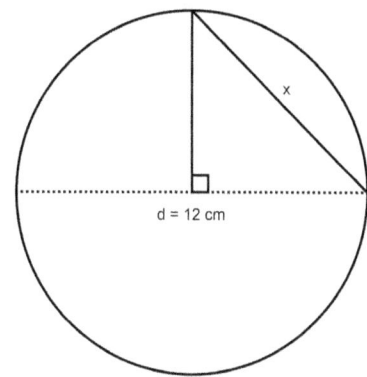

Note: Figure not drawn to scale

47. Calculate the length of side x.

a. 6.46
b. 8.48
c. 3.6
d. 6.4

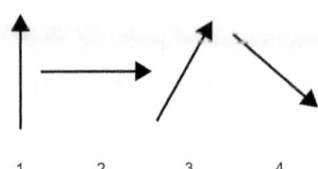

1 2 3 4

48. What is the correct order of respective slopes for the lines above?

    a. Positive, undefined, negative, positive
    b. Negative, zero, undefined, positive
    c. Undefined, zero, positive, negative
    d. Zero, positive undefined, negative

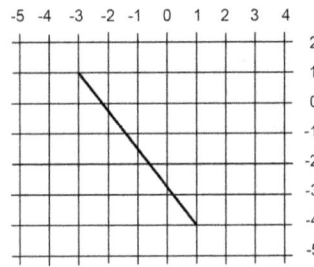

49. What is the slope of the line shown above?

    a. 5/4
    b. -4/5
    c. -5/4
    d. -4/5

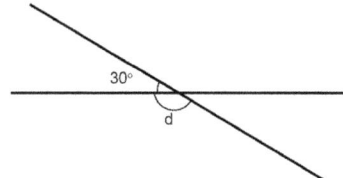

50. What is the indicated angle above?

    a. 150°
    b. 330°
    c. 60°
    d. 120°

Answer Key

Section 1 – Reading

1. B
We can infer from this passage that sickness from an infectious disease can be easily transmitted from one person to another.

From the passage, "Infectious pathologies are also called communicable diseases or transmissible diseases, due to their potential of transmission from one person or species to another by a replicating agent (as opposed to a toxin)."

2. A
Two other names for infectious pathologies are communicable diseases and transmissible diseases.

From the passage, "Infectious pathologies are also called communicable diseases or transmissible diseases, due to their potential of transmission from one person or species to another by a replicating agent (as opposed to a toxin)."

3. C
Infectivity describes the ability of an organism to enter, survive and multiply in the host. This is taken directly from the passage, and is a definition type question.

Definition type questions can be answered quickly and easily by scanning the passage for the word you are asked to define.

"Infectivity" is an unusual word, so it is quick and easy to scan the passage looking for this word.

4. B
We know an infection is not synonymous with an infectious disease because an infection may not cause important clinical symptoms or impair host function.

5. C
The cumulus stage of a thunderstorm is the beginning of the thunderstorm.

This is taken directly from the passage, "The first stage of a thunderstorm is the cumulus, or developing stage."

6. D
The passage lists four ways that air is heated. One of the ways is, heat created by water vapor condensing into liquid.

7. A
The sequence of events can be taken from these sentences:

As the moisture carried by the [1] air currents rises, it rapidly cools into liquid drops of water, which appear as cumulus clouds. As the water vapor condenses into liquid, it [2] releases heat, which warms the air. This in turn, causes the air to become less dense than the surrounding dry air and [3] rise farther.

8. C
The purpose of this text is to explain when meteorologists consider a thunderstorm severe.

The main idea is the first sentence, "The United States National Weather Service classifies thunderstorms as severe when they reach a predetermined level." After the first sentence, the passage explains and elaborates on this idea. Everything is this passage is related to this idea, and there are no other major ideas in this passage that are central to the whole passage.

9. A
From this passage, we can infer that different areas and countries have different criteria for determining a severe storm.

From the passage we can see that most of the US has a criteria of, winds over 50 knots (58 mph or 93 km/h), and hail ¾ inch (2 cm). For the Central US, hail must be 1 inch (2.5 cm) in diameter. In Canada, winds must be 90 km/h or greater, hail 2 centimeters in diameter or greater, and rainfall more than 50 millimeters in 1 hour, or 75 millimeters in 3 hours.

Choice D is incorrect because the Canadian system is the same for hail, 2 centimeters in diameter.

10. C
With hail above the minimum size of 2.5 cm. diameter, the Central Region of the United States National Weather Service would issue a severe thunderstorm warning.

11. C
You would find information about natural selection and adaptation in the ecology section which begins on page 110.

12. D
Clouds in space are made of different materials attracted by gravity. Clouds on Earth are made of water droplets or ice crystals.

Choice D is the best answer. Notice also that Choice D is the most specific.

13. C
The main idea is the first sentence of the passage; a cloud is a visible mass of droplets or frozen crystals floating in the atmosphere above the surface of the Earth or other planetary body.

The main idea is very often the first sentence of the paragraph.

14. C
This question asks about the process, and gives choices that can be confirmed or eliminated easily.

From the passage, "Dense, deep clouds reflect most light, so they appear white, at least from the top. Cloud droplets scatter light very efficiently, so the farther into a cloud light travels, the weaker it gets. This accounts for the gray or dark appearance at the base of large clouds."

We can eliminate choice A, since water droplets inside the

cloud do not reflect light is false.

We can eliminate choice B, since, water droplets outside the cloud reflect light, it appears dark, is false.

Choice C is correct.

15. A
The correct order of ingredients is brown sugar, baking soda and chocolate chips.

16. B
Sturdy: strong, solid in structure or person. In context, Stir in chocolate chips by hand with a *sturdy* wooden spoon.

17. A
Disperse: to scatter in different directions or break up. In context, Stir until the chocolate chips and nuts are evenly *dispersed*.

18. B
You can stop stirring the nuts when they are evenly distributed. From the passage, "Stir until the chocolate chips and nuts are evenly dispersed."

19. B
Reading the document posted to the Human Resources website is optional.

20. B
The document is recommended changes and have not be implemented yet.

21. A
Navy SEALs are the maritime component of the United States Special Operations Command (USSOCOM).

22. C
Working underwater separates SEALs from other military units. This is taken directly from the passage.

23. D
SEALs also belong to the Navy and the Coast Guard.

24. A
The CIA also participated. From the passage, the raid was conducted by a "team of 40 *CIA-led* Navy SEALS."

25. C
From the passage, "The Navy SEALs were part of the Naval Special Warfare Development Group, previously called "Team 6."

26. A
The sentence is a recommendation.

27. C
Tips for a good night's sleep is the best alternative title for this article.

28. B
Mental activity is helpful for a good night's sleep is can not be inferred from this article.

29. A
The Save the Children's fund has raised $12,000 out of $20,000, or 12/20. Simplifying, 12/20 = 3/5

30. B
The Save the Children's fund has raised $12,000 out of $16,000, or 12/16. Simplifying, 12/16 = 3/4

Vocabulary

31. C
Dauntless: adj. Invulnerable to fear or intimidation.

32. A
Juxtaposed: adj. Placed side-by-side often for comparison or contrast.

33. B
Regicide: v. killing of a king.

34. A
Pernicious: adj. Causing much harm in a subtle way.

35. A
Immune: adj. Resistant to a particular infection or toxin owing to the presence of specific antibodies.

36. B
Nimble: adj. Quick and light in movement or action.

37. A
Queries: n. Questions or inquiries.

38. C
Depose: To remove (a leader) from (high) office, without killing the incumbent.

39. D
Pedestrian: Ordinary, dull; everyday; unexceptional.

40. B
Petulant: adj. Childishly irritable.

41. D
Pesticide: n. A substance used for destroying insects or other organisms harmful to cultivated plants or to animals.

42. D
Salient: adj. worthy or note or relevant.

43. B
Sedentary: adj. not moving or sitting in one place.

44. A
Famine: n. extreme scarcity of food.

45. A
Stint: n. To be sparing.

46. A
Precipitate: v. to rain.

47. C
Edify: v. To instruct or improve morally or intellectually.

48. B
Egress: n. An exit or way out.

49. A
Recede: v. To move back, to move away.

50. A
Confidential: adj. kept secret within a certain circle of persons; not intended to be known publicly.

English Language Arts Answer Key

1. C
Comma separate phrases.

2. D
The comma separates clauses and numbers are separated with a comma. The correct sentence is,
'To travel around the globe, you have to drive 25,000 miles.'

3. A
The dog loved chasing bones, but never ate them; it was running that he enjoyed.

4. B
The semicolon links independent clauses with a conjunction (therefore).

5. D
The third conditional is used for talking about an unreal situation (that did not happen) in the past. For example, "If I had studied harder, [if clause] I would have passed the exam [main clause]. Which is the same as, "I failed the exam, because I didn't study hard enough."

6. C
Double negative sentence. In double negative sentences, one of the negatives is replaced with "any."

7. A
Disagreeing with a negative statement uses "neither." Disagreeing with a negative statement uses "neither." Use "I do" and "He does."

8. C
Doesn't, does not, or does is used with the third person singular--words like he, she, and it. Don't, do not, or do is used for other subjects.

9. C
Bring vs. Take. Usage depends on your location. Something coming your way is brought to you. Something going away is taken from you.

10. C
Present perfect. You cannot use the Present Perfect with specific time expressions such as: yesterday, one year ago, last week, when I was a child, at that moment, that day, one day, etc. The Present Perfect is used with unspecific expressions such as: ever, never, once, many times, several times, before, so far, already, yet, etc.

11. C
Fewer vs. Less. 'Fewer' is used with countables and 'less' is used with uncountables.

12. B
Went vs. Gone. Went is the simple past tense. Gone is used in the past perfect.

13. A
When using 'however,' place a comma before and after, except when however begins the sentence.

14. C
Its vs. It's. 'It's' is a contraction for it is or it has. 'Its' is a possessive pronoun meaning, more or less, of it or belonging to it.

15. C
Lay vs. Lie. Lie requires an object and lay does not. Laid is the past tense of lay.

16. D
The third conditional is used for talking about an unreal situation (that did not happen) in the past. For example, "If I had studied harder, [if clause] I would have passed the exam [main clause]. Which is the same as, "I failed the exam, because I didn't study hard enough."

17. D
A vs. An. The article 'a' come before a consonant and 'an' comes before a vowel.

18. A
Accept vs. Except. To accept is to receive or to say yes. Except is a preposition that means excluding.

19. A
Advise vs. Advice. To advise is to give advice. Advice is an opinion that someone offers.

20. C
Adapt vs. Adopt.
Adapt means "to change." Usually we adapt to someone or something. Adopt means "to take as one's own."

21. D
Among vs. Between. 'Among' is for more than 2 items, and 'between' is only for 2 items.

When he's among friends (many or more than 2), Robert seems confident, but, between you and me (two), he is very shy.

22. D
At vs. About. At refers to a specific time and about refers to a more general time. A common usage is 'at about 10,' but it isn't proper grammar.

23. B
Beside vs. Besides. 'Beside' means next to, and 'besides' means in addition to.

24. A
Can vs. May. 'Can' refers to ability and 'may' refers to permission.

Although John can swim (is able to. very well, he may not (permission. be allowed to swim in the pool.

25. B
Continual vs. Continuous. 'Continuous' means a time with no interruption and 'continual' means a time with interruption.

Her continual absences (with interruption – not always absent) caused a continuous disruption (the disruption was ongoing without interruption) at the office.

26. A
Emigrate vs. Immigrate. To emigrate means to leave one's country and to immigrate means to come to a country.

27. B
Further vs. Farther. 'Farther' is used for physical distance, and 'further' is used for figurative distance.

28. B
Former vs. Latter. 'Former' refers to the first of two things, 'latter' to the second.

29. A
Sit vs. Set. 'Set' requires an object – something to set down. 'Sit' is something that you do, like sit on the chair.

30. C
The names of God, specific deities, religious figures, and holy books are capitalized.

31. B
Capitalize a title when used with a name or other noun. So, The Mayor of Chicago is capitalized, whereas "he spoke to the mayor" is not.

32. B
Titles preceding names are capitalized, but not titles that follow names.

33. C
Holidays are capitalized, the names of seasons are not.

34. C
The names of seasons are not capitalized because they are generic nouns. If a season is used in a title, such as the "Fall 2012 semester," Fall 2012 is a title and capitalized.

35. A
A Pronoun should conform to its antecedent in gender, number and person.

36. A
The verb LAY should always take an object. Here the subject is the table. The three forms of the verb lay are: lay, laid and laid. The sentence above is in past tense.

37. B
Use the singular verb form when nouns are qualified with "every" or "each," even if they are joined by 'and.'

38. B
The sentence is correct. Use a plural verb for nouns like measles, tongs, trousers, riches, scissors etc.

39. B
Use "could," the past tense of "can" to express ability or capacity.

40. C
The sentence is correct. Words such as neither, each, many, either, every, everyone, everybody and any should take a singular pronoun.

41. A
The verb "ought" can be used to express desirability, duty and probability. The verb is usually followed by "to."

42. A
When two subjects are linked with "with" or "as well," use the verb form that matches the first subject.

43. A
When you use 'each other' it should be used for two things or people. When you use 'one another' it should be used for things and people above two

44. B
The verb rise ('to go up', 'to ascend.') can appear in three forms, rise, rose, and risen. The verb should not take an object.

45. A
The sentence is correct. Use "whom" in the objective case, and use "who" a subjective case.

46. C
Always use the singular verb form for nouns like politics, wages, mathematics, innings, news, advice, summons, furniture, information, poetry, machinery, vacation, scenery etc.

47. B
Use a singular verb with a proper noun in plural form that refers to a single entity. Here the The World Health Organization is a single entity, although it is made up on many members.

48. A
Will is used in the second or third person (they, he, she and you), while shall is used in the first person (I and we). Both verbs are used to express futurity.

MATHEMATICS

1. B
Six times a number plus five is the same as saying six times (a number plus five). Or,
6 * (a number plus five). Let X be the number so, 6(X+5).

2. A
Three plus a number times 7 equals 42. Let X be the number. (3 + X) times 7 = 42
7(3 + X) = 42

3. C
If there are 5 friends and each drink costs $1.89, we can round up to $2 per drink and estimate the total cost at, 5 X $2 = $10.

The actual cost is 5 X $1.89 = $9.45.

4. B
Estimate 215 X 65. First start with 200 X 50, which is 10,000, so the answer will be about 10,000. The only choice that is close is 13,500, choice B.

5. A
The graph shows oil consumption peaked in 2011.

6. A
The sample space of this event will be S = { (H,1),(H,2),(H,3),(H,4),(H,5),(H,6) (T,1),(T,2),(T,3),(T,4),(T,5),(T,6) } So there are a total of 12 outcomes and 8 winning outcomes. The probability of a win in a single event is P (W) =8/12=2/3. In 20 games the probability of a win = 2/3 × 20 = 13.53, or about 13.

7. D
Let us denote Sarah's weight by "x." Then, since she weighs 25 pounds more than Tony, Tony will be x-25. They together weigh 205 pounds which means that the sum of the two representations will be equal to 205:

Sarah : x

Tony : x - 25

x + (x - 25) = 205 ... by arranging this equation we have:

x + x - 25 = 205

2x - 25 = 205 ... we add 25 to each side to have x term alone:

2x - 25 + 25 = 205 + 25

2x = 230

x = 230/2

x = 115 pounds → Sarah weighs 115 pounds. Since 1 pound is 0.4535 kilograms, we need to multiply 115 by 0.4535 to have her weight in kilograms:

x = 115 • 0.4535 = 52.1525 kilograms → this is equal to 52 when rounded to the nearest whole number.

8. B
The line is pointing towards numbers less than 1. The equation is therefore, X < 1.

9. C
$243/3^3$ 3 x 3 x 3 = 27
243/27 = 9

10. D
75/1500 = 15/300 = 3/60 = 1/20

11. B

Day	Number of Absent Students	Number of Present Students	% Attendance
Monday	5	40	88.88%
Tuesday	9	36	80.00%
Wednesday	4	41	91.11%
Thursday	10	35	77.77%
Friday	6	39	86.66%

88.88 + 80.00 + 91.11 + 77.77 + 86.66/5

424.42/5 = 84.88
Round up to 85%.

Percentage attendance will be 85%

12. D
2/3 - 2/5 = 10 - 6 /15 = 4/15

13. D
Comparing respective angles - 70°, 75°, 35°

14. C
Equilateral triangle with 9 cm. sides
Perimeter = 9 + 9 + 9 = 27 cm.

15. C
0.27 + 0.33 = 0.60 and 0.60 = 60/100 = 3/5

16. B
(7 x 7 x 7 x 7 x 7) - (3 x 3 x 3 x 3 x 3) = 16,807 – 243 = 16,564

17. B
2/4 X 3/4 = 6/16, and lowest terms = 3/8

18. B
4y + 24 = 3y + 30, = 4y – 3y + 24 = 30, = y + 24 = 30, = y = 30 – 24, = y = 6

19. B
2/3 x 60 = 40 and 1/5 x 75 = 15, 40 + 15 = 55.

20. D
Perimeter of triangle ABC is asked.
Perimeter of a triangle = sum of all three sides.

Here, Perimeter of ΔABC = |AC| + |CB| + |AB|.

Since the triangle is located in the middle of two adjacent and identical rectangles, we find the side lengths using these rectangles:

|AB| = 6 + 6 = 12 cm

|CB| = 8.5 cm

|AC| = |CB| = 8.5 cm

Perimeter = |AC| + |CB| + |AB| = 8.5 + 8.5 + 12 = 29 cm

21. D
3.13 + 7.87 = 11 and 11 X 5 = 55

22. A
10 x 10 x 100 x 100 = 1000^x, =100 x 10,000 = 1000^x, = 1,000,000 = 1000^x = x = 2

23. A
1/3 X 3/4 = 3/12 = 1/4

24. B
a + b + c + d = ?
The sum of angles around a point is 360°
a + b + c + d = 360°

25. A
5^6

26. C
Exponential form is 9^3 and standard from is 729

27. B
$(4)(3)^3$ = (4)(27) = 108

28. B
0.524/ 10 x 10 x 10 = 0.524/1000 = 0.000524

29. B
X = 7, so 3x = 3 x 7 = 21, 2x = 2 x 7 = 14, so 21 + 5 - 14 = 26 - 14 = 12

30. C
There are two fractions containing x and the denominators are different. First, let us find a common denominator to simplify the expression. The least common multiplier of 4 and 7 is 28. Then,
7(x – 2) / 28 – 4(3x + 5) / 28 = -3.28 / 28 ... Since both sides are written on the denominator 28 now, we can eliminate them:
7(x – 2) – 4(3x + 5) = -84

7x – 14 – 12x – 20 = -84
-5x = - 84 + 14 + 20
-5x = - 50
x = 50/5
x = 10

31. C
2/7 + 2/3 = 6+14 /21 (21 is the common denominator) = 20/21

32. D
When multiplying exponents with the same base, add the exponents. $3^2 \times 3^5 = 3^{2+5} = 3^7$

33. A
The wheel travels 2πr distance when it makes one revolution. Here, r stands for the radius. The radius is given as 25 cm in the figure. So,

2πr = 2π * 25 = 50π cm is the distance travelled in one revolution.

In 175 revolutions: 175 * 50π = 8750π cm is travelled.

We are asked to find the distance in meter.

1 m = 100 cm So;

8750π cm = 8750π / 100 = 87.5π m

34. A
Multiply the first bracket and the second. x^2 - 3x + 7x -21= x^2 + 4x – 21

35. D
2009 X 108 = 216,972. This is an easy question to guess. 2000 X 100 = 200,000, so choices A, B and C can be eliminated right away.

36. A
Black stone for 200 tiles = 200 x [Total tile area – Inner white area(4 triangles)]
= 200 x [(16^2)-(4 x 1/2 x 8 x 8)] = 200 x (256 - 128) = 200 x 128 = 25600 cm^2
Converting to meters – 1 cm. = 0.01 meters

= 25600/100 m²
= 256 m²

37. B
0.27 (9 x 9) = 0.27 x 81 = 21.87

38. B
She spent 15% - 100% - 15% = 85%

39. A
If a line represents an equation, all points on that line should satisfy the equation. Meaning that all (x, y) pairs present on the line should be able to verify that 2y - x is equal to 4. We can find out the correct line by trying a (x, y) point existing on each line. It is easier to choose points on the intersection of the gridlines:

Let us try the point (4, 4) on line A:

2 * 4 - 4 = 4

8 - 4 = 4

4 = 4 ... this is a correct result, so the equation for line A is 2y - x = 4.

Let us try other points to check the other lines:

Point (-1, 2) on line B:

2 * 2 - (-1) = 4

4 + 1 = 4

5 = 4 ... this is a wrong result, so the equation for line B is not 2y - x = 4.

Point (3, -1) on line C:

2 * (-1) - 3 = 4

-2 - 3 = 4

-5 = 4 ... this is a wrong result, so the equation for line C is not 2y - x = 4.

Point (-2, -1) on line D:

2 * (-1) - (-2) = 4

-2 + 2 = 4

0 = 4 ... this is a wrong result, so the equation for line D is not 2y - x = 4.

40. C
The sum of angles around a point is 360°
d + 300 = 360°
d = 60°

41. A
Find the perimeter of a shape made by merging a square and a semi circle. Perimeter = 3 sides of the square + 1/2 circumference of the circle.
= (3 x 5) + 1/2 (5 π)
= 15 + 2.5 π
= 15 + 7.853975
Perimeter = 22.85 cm

42. A
$3^{8-5} = 3^3$
To divide exponents with the same base, subtract the exponents.

43. C
3x = 27, x = 27/3, x = 9

44. A
If we call one side of the square "a," the area of the square will be a^2.

We know that a^2 = 200 cm².

On the other hand; there is an isosceles right triangle. Using the **Pythagorean Theorem:**

(Hypotenuse)² = (Adjacent Side)² + (Opposite Side)² Where the hypotenuse is equal to one side of the square. So,

$a^2 = x^2 + x^2$

$200 = 2x^2$

$200/2 = 2x^2/2$

$100 = x^2$

$x = \sqrt{100}$

$x = 10$ cm

45. D
$3b + 5b - 4, = 8b - 4, = 8b = 4, b = 4/8, = b = ½$

46. D
$3.14 + 2.73 = 5.87$ and $5.87 + 23.7 = 29.57$

47. B
In the question, we have a right triangle formed inside the circle. We are asked to find the length of the hypotenuse of this triangle. We can find the other two sides of the triangle by using circle properties:

The diameter of the circle is equal to 12 cm. The legs of the right triangle are the radii of the circle; so they are 6 cm long.

Using the Pythagorean Theorem:

(Hypotenuse)² = (Adjacent Side)² + (Opposite Side)²

$x^2 = r^2 + r^2$

$x^2 = 6^2 + 6^2$

$x^2 = 72$

$x = \sqrt{72}$

$x = 8.48$

48. C
Undefined, zero, positive, negative.

49. C
Slope (m) = change in y
            change in x

$(x_1, y_1) = (-3, 1)$ & $(x_2, y_2) = (1, -4)$
Slope = $[-4 - 1]/[1-(-3)] = -5/4$

50. A

The angles opposite both angles 30° and angle d are respectively equal to vertical angles.

$2(30° + d) = 360°$

$2d = 360° - 60°$

$2d = 300°$

$d = 150°$

Practice Test Questions Set 2

THE PRACTICE TEST PORTION PRESENTS QUESTIONS THAT ARE REPRESENTATIVE OF THE TYPE OF QUESTION YOU SHOULD EXPECT TO FIND ON THE CHSPE. However, they are not intended to match exactly what is on the CHSPE.

For the best results, take this Practice Test as if it were the real exam. Set aside time when you will not be disturbed, and a location that is quiet and free of distractions. Read the instructions carefully, read each question carefully, and answer to the best of your ability.

Use the bubble answer sheets provided. When you have completed the Practice Test, check your answer against the Answer Key and read the explanation provided.

Reading Answer Sheet

1. Ⓐ Ⓑ Ⓒ Ⓓ
2. Ⓐ Ⓑ Ⓒ Ⓓ
3. Ⓐ Ⓑ Ⓒ Ⓓ
4. Ⓐ Ⓑ Ⓒ Ⓓ
5. Ⓐ Ⓑ Ⓒ Ⓓ
6. Ⓐ Ⓑ Ⓒ Ⓓ
7. Ⓐ Ⓑ Ⓒ Ⓓ
8. Ⓐ Ⓑ Ⓒ Ⓓ
9. Ⓐ Ⓑ Ⓒ Ⓓ
10. Ⓐ Ⓑ Ⓒ Ⓓ
11. Ⓐ Ⓑ Ⓒ Ⓓ
12. Ⓐ Ⓑ Ⓒ Ⓓ
13. Ⓐ Ⓑ Ⓒ Ⓓ
14. Ⓐ Ⓑ Ⓒ Ⓓ
15. Ⓐ Ⓑ Ⓒ Ⓓ
16. Ⓐ Ⓑ Ⓒ Ⓓ
17. Ⓐ Ⓑ Ⓒ Ⓓ
18. Ⓐ Ⓑ Ⓒ Ⓓ
19. Ⓐ Ⓑ Ⓒ Ⓓ
20. Ⓐ Ⓑ Ⓒ Ⓓ
21. Ⓐ Ⓑ Ⓒ Ⓓ
22. Ⓐ Ⓑ Ⓒ Ⓓ
23. Ⓐ Ⓑ Ⓒ Ⓓ
24. Ⓐ Ⓑ Ⓒ Ⓓ
25. Ⓐ Ⓑ Ⓒ Ⓓ
26. Ⓐ Ⓑ Ⓒ Ⓓ
27. Ⓐ Ⓑ Ⓒ Ⓓ
28. Ⓐ Ⓑ Ⓒ Ⓓ
29. Ⓐ Ⓑ Ⓒ Ⓓ
30. Ⓐ Ⓑ Ⓒ Ⓓ
31. Ⓐ Ⓑ Ⓒ Ⓓ
32. Ⓐ Ⓑ Ⓒ Ⓓ
33. Ⓐ Ⓑ Ⓒ Ⓓ
34. Ⓐ Ⓑ Ⓒ Ⓓ
35. Ⓐ Ⓑ Ⓒ Ⓓ
36. Ⓐ Ⓑ Ⓒ Ⓓ
37. Ⓐ Ⓑ Ⓒ Ⓓ
38. Ⓐ Ⓑ Ⓒ Ⓓ
39. Ⓐ Ⓑ Ⓒ Ⓓ
40. Ⓐ Ⓑ Ⓒ Ⓓ
41. Ⓐ Ⓑ Ⓒ Ⓓ
42. Ⓐ Ⓑ Ⓒ Ⓓ
43. Ⓐ Ⓑ Ⓒ Ⓓ
44. Ⓐ Ⓑ Ⓒ Ⓓ
45. Ⓐ Ⓑ Ⓒ Ⓓ
46. Ⓐ Ⓑ Ⓒ Ⓓ
47. Ⓐ Ⓑ Ⓒ Ⓓ
48. Ⓐ Ⓑ Ⓒ Ⓓ
49. Ⓐ Ⓑ Ⓒ Ⓓ
50. Ⓐ Ⓑ Ⓒ Ⓓ

English and Language Arts Answer Sheet

1. A B C D
2. A B C D
3. A B C D
4. A B C D
5. A B C D
6. A B C D
7. A B C D
8. A B C D
9. A B C D
10. A B C D
11. A B C D
12. A B C D
13. A B C D
14. A B C D
15. A B C D
16. A B C D
17. A B C D
18. A B C D
19. A B C D
20. A B C D
21. A B C D
22. A B C D
23. A B C D
24. A B C D
25. A B C D
26. A B C D
27. A B C D
28. A B C D
29. A B C D
30. A B C D
31. A B C D
32. A B C D
33. A B C D
34. A B C D
35. A B C D
36. A B C D
37. A B C D
38. A B C D
39. A B C D
40. A B C D
41. A B C D
42. A B C D
43. A B C D
44. A B C D
45. A B C D
46. A B C D
47. A B C D
48. A B C D
49. A B C D
50. A B C D

Mathematics Answer Sheet

1. Ⓐ Ⓑ Ⓒ Ⓓ
2. Ⓐ Ⓑ Ⓒ Ⓓ
3. Ⓐ Ⓑ Ⓒ Ⓓ
4. Ⓐ Ⓑ Ⓒ Ⓓ
5. Ⓐ Ⓑ Ⓒ Ⓓ
6. Ⓐ Ⓑ Ⓒ Ⓓ
7. Ⓐ Ⓑ Ⓒ Ⓓ
8. Ⓐ Ⓑ Ⓒ Ⓓ
9. Ⓐ Ⓑ Ⓒ Ⓓ
10. Ⓐ Ⓑ Ⓒ Ⓓ
11. Ⓐ Ⓑ Ⓒ Ⓓ
12. Ⓐ Ⓑ Ⓒ Ⓓ
13. Ⓐ Ⓑ Ⓒ Ⓓ
14. Ⓐ Ⓑ Ⓒ Ⓓ
15. Ⓐ Ⓑ Ⓒ Ⓓ
16. Ⓐ Ⓑ Ⓒ Ⓓ
17. Ⓐ Ⓑ Ⓒ Ⓓ
18. Ⓐ Ⓑ Ⓒ Ⓓ
19. Ⓐ Ⓑ Ⓒ Ⓓ
20. Ⓐ Ⓑ Ⓒ Ⓓ
21. Ⓐ Ⓑ Ⓒ Ⓓ
22. Ⓐ Ⓑ Ⓒ Ⓓ
23. Ⓐ Ⓑ Ⓒ Ⓓ
24. Ⓐ Ⓑ Ⓒ Ⓓ
25. Ⓐ Ⓑ Ⓒ Ⓓ
26. Ⓐ Ⓑ Ⓒ Ⓓ
27. Ⓐ Ⓑ Ⓒ Ⓓ
28. Ⓐ Ⓑ Ⓒ Ⓓ
29. Ⓐ Ⓑ Ⓒ Ⓓ
30. Ⓐ Ⓑ Ⓒ Ⓓ
31. Ⓐ Ⓑ Ⓒ Ⓓ
32. Ⓐ Ⓑ Ⓒ Ⓓ
33. Ⓐ Ⓑ Ⓒ Ⓓ
34. Ⓐ Ⓑ Ⓒ Ⓓ
35. Ⓐ Ⓑ Ⓒ Ⓓ
36. Ⓐ Ⓑ Ⓒ Ⓓ
37. Ⓐ Ⓑ Ⓒ Ⓓ
38. Ⓐ Ⓑ Ⓒ Ⓓ
39. Ⓐ Ⓑ Ⓒ Ⓓ
40. Ⓐ Ⓑ Ⓒ Ⓓ
41. Ⓐ Ⓑ Ⓒ Ⓓ
42. Ⓐ Ⓑ Ⓒ Ⓓ
43. Ⓐ Ⓑ Ⓒ Ⓓ
44. Ⓐ Ⓑ Ⓒ Ⓓ
45. Ⓐ Ⓑ Ⓒ Ⓓ
46. Ⓐ Ⓑ Ⓒ Ⓓ
47. Ⓐ Ⓑ Ⓒ Ⓓ
48. Ⓐ Ⓑ Ⓒ Ⓓ
49. Ⓐ Ⓑ Ⓒ Ⓓ
50. Ⓐ Ⓑ Ⓒ Ⓓ

Reading and Language Arts

Questions 1-4 refer to the following passage.

The Respiratory System

The respiratory system's function is to allow oxygen exchange through all parts of the body. The anatomy or structure of the exchange system, and the uses of the exchanged gases, varies depending on the organism. In humans and other mammals, for example, the anatomical features of the respiratory system include airways, lungs, and the respiratory muscles. Molecules of oxygen and carbon dioxide are passively exchanged, by diffusion, between the gaseous external environment and the blood. This exchange process occurs in the alveolar region of the lungs.

Other animals, such as insects, have respiratory systems with very simple anatomical features, and in amphibians even the skin plays a vital role in gas exchange. Plants also have respiratory systems but the direction of gas exchange can be opposite to that of animals.

The respiratory system can also be divided into physiological, or functional, zones. These include the conducting zone (the region for gas transport from the outside atmosphere to just above the alveoli), the transitional zone, and the respiratory zone (the alveolar region where gas exchange occurs). [8]

1. What can we infer from the first paragraph in this passage?

    a. Human and mammal respiratory systems are the same

    b. The lungs are an important part of the respiratory system

    c. The respiratory system varies in different mammals

    d. Oxygen and carbon dioxide are passive exchanged by the respiratory system

2. What is the process by which molecules of oxygen and carbon dioxide are passively exchanged?

   a. Transfusion
   b. Affusion
   c. Diffusion
   d. Respiratory confusion

3. What organ plays an important role in gas exchange in amphibians?

   a. The skin
   b. The lungs
   c. The gills
   d. The mouth

4. What are the three physiological zones of the respiratory system?

   a. Conducting, transitional, respiratory zones
   b. Redacting, transitional, circulatory zones
   c. Conducting, circulatory, inhibiting zones
   d. Transitional, inhibiting, conducting zones

Questions 5-8 refer to the following passage.

ABC Electric Warranty

ABC Electric Company warrants that its products are free from defects in material and workmanship. Subject to the conditions and limitations set forth below, ABC Electric will, at its option, either repair or replace any part of its products that prove defective due to improper workmanship or materials.

This limited warranty does not cover any damage to the product from improper installation, accident, abuse, misuse, natural disaster, insufficient or excessive electrical supply, abnormal mechanical or environmental conditions, or any unauthorized disassembly, repair, or modification.

This limited warranty also does not apply to any product on which the original identification information has been altered, or removed, has not been handled or packaged correctly, or has been sold as second-hand.

This limited warranty covers only repair, replacement, refund or credit for defective ABC Electric products, as provided above.

5. I tried to repair my ABC Electric blender, but could not, so can I get it repaired under this warranty?

    a. Yes, the warranty still covers the blender

    b. No, the warranty does not cover the blender

    c. Uncertain. ABC Electric may or may not cover repairs under this warranty

6. My ABC Electric fan is not working. Will ABC Electric provide a new one or repair this one?

    a. ABC Electric will repair my fan

    b. ABC Electric will replace my fan

    c. ABC Electric could either replace or repair my fan

    I can request either a replacement or a repair.

7. My stove was damaged in a flood. Does this warranty cover my stove?

    a. Yes, it is covered.

    b. No, it is not covered.

    c. It may or may not be covered.

    d. ABC Electric will decide if it is covered

8. Which of the following is an example of improper workmanship?

    a. Missing parts
    b. Defective parts
    c. Scratches on the front
    d. None of the above

Questions 9 - 12 refer to the following passage.

Low Blood Sugar

As the name suggest, low blood sugar is low sugar levels in the bloodstream. This can occur when you have not eaten properly and undertake strenuous activity, or when you are very hungry. When low blood sugar occurs regularly and is ongoing, it is a medical condition called hypoglycemia. This condition can occur in diabetics and in healthy adults.

Causes of low blood sugar can include excessive alcohol consumption, metabolic problems, stomach surgery, pancreas, liver or kidneys problems, as well as a side-effect of some medications.

Symptoms

There are different symptoms depending on the severity of the case.

Mild hypoglycemia can lead to feelings of nausea and hunger. The patient may also feel nervous, jittery and have fast heart beats. Sweaty skin, clammy and cold skin are likely symptoms.

Moderate hypoglycemia can result in a short temper, confusion, nervousness, fear and blurring of vision. The patient may feel weak and unsteady.

Severe cases of hypoglycemia can lead to seizures, coma, fainting spells, nightmares, headaches, excessive sweats and severe tiredness.

Diagnosis of low blood sugar

A doctor can diagnosis this medical condition by asking the patient questions and testing blood and urine samples. Home testing kits are available for patients to monitor blood sugar levels. It is important to see a qualified doctor though. The doctor can administer tests to ensure that will safely rule out other medical conditions that could affect blood sugar levels.

Treatment

Quick treatments include drinking or eating foods and drinks with high sugar contents. Good examples include soda, fruit juice, hard candy and raisins. Glucose energy tablets can also help. Doctors may also recommend medications and well as changes in diet and exercise routine to treat chronic low blood sugar.

9. Based on the article, which of the following is true?

    a. Low blood sugar can happen to anyone.

    b. Low blood sugar only happens to diabetics.

    c. Low blood sugar can occur even.

    d. None of the statements are true.

10. Which of the following are the author's opinion?

    a. Quick treatments include drinking or eating foods and drinks with high sugar contents.

    b. None of the statements are opinions.

    c. This condition can occur in diabetics and in healthy adults.

    d. There are different symptoms depending on the severity of the case

11. What is the author's purpose?

    a. To inform

    b. To persuade

    c. To entertain

    d. To analyze

12. Which of the following is not a detail?

    a. A doctor can diagnosis this medical condition by asking the patient questions and testing.

    b. A doctor will test blood and urine samples.

    c. Glucose energy tablets can also help.

    d. Home test kits monitor blood sugar levels.

Chapter 1 - Getting Started

    A Better Score Is Possible 6
    Types of Multiple Choice 9
    Multiple Choice Step-by-Step 12
    Tips for Reading the Instructions 13
    General Multiple Choice Tips 14
    Multiple Choice Strategy Practice 20
    Answer Key 39

13. Based on the partial Table of Contents above, what is this book about?

    a. How to answer multiple choice questions

    b. Different types of multiple choice questions

    c. How to write a test

    d. None of the above

Questions 14-17 refer to the following passage.

Myths, Legend and Folklore

Cultural historians draw a distinction between myth, legend and folktale simply as a way to group traditional stories. However, in many cultures, drawing a sharp line between myths and legends is not that simple. Instead of dividing their traditional stories into myths, legends, and folktales, some cultures divide them into two categories. The first category roughly corresponds to folktales, and the second is one that combines myths and legends. Similarly, we can not always separate myths from folktales. One society might consider a story true, making it a myth. Another society may believe the story is fiction, which makes it a folktale. In fact, when a myth loses its status as part of a religious system, it often takes on traits more typical of folktales, with its formerly divine characters now appearing as human heroes, giants, or fairies. Myth, legend, and folktale are only a few of the categories of traditional stories. Other categories include anecdotes and some kinds of jokes. Traditional stories, in turn, are only one category within the larger category of folklore, which also includes items such as gestures, costumes, and music. [9]

14. The main idea of this passage is that

a. Myths, fables, and folktales are not the same thing, and each describes a specific type of story

b. Traditional stories can be categorized in different ways by different people

c. Cultures use myths for religious purposes, and when this is no longer true, the people forget and discard these myths

d. Myths can never become folk tales, because one is true, and the other is false

15. The terms myth and legend are

   a. Categories that are synonymous with true and false

   b. Categories that group traditional stories according to certain characteristics

   c. Interchangeable, because both terms mean a story that is passed down from generation to generation

   d. Meant to distinguish between a story that involves a hero and a cultural message and a story meant only to entertain

16. Traditional story categories not only include myths and legends, but

   a. Can also include gestures, since some cultures passed these down before the written and spoken word

   b. In addition, folklore refers to stories involving fables and fairy tales

   c. These story categories can also include folk music and traditional dress

   d. Traditional stories themselves are a part of the larger category of folklore, which may also include costumes, gestures, and music

17. This passage shows that

   a. There is a distinct difference between a myth and a legend, although both are folktales

   b. Myths are folktales, but folktales are not myths

   c. Myths, legends, and folktales play an important part in tradition and the past, and are a rich and colorful part of history

   d. Most cultures consider myths to be true

Questions 18 - 20 refer to the following passage.

Lowest Price Guarantee

Get it for less. Guaranteed!

ABC Electric will beat any advertised price by 10% of the difference.

> 1) If you find a lower advertised price, we will beat it by 10% of the difference.
>
> 2) If you find a lower advertised price within 30 days* of your purchase we will beat it by 10% of the difference.
>
> 3) If our own price is reduced within 30 days* of your purchase, bring in your receipt and we will refund the difference.

*14 days for computers, monitors, printers, laptops, tablets, cellular & wireless devices, home security products, projectors, camcorders, digital cameras, radar detectors, portable DVD players, DJ and pro-audio equipment, and air conditioners.

18. I bought a radar detector 15 days ago and saw an ad for the same model only cheaper. Can I get 10% of the difference refunded?

> a. Yes. Since it is less than 30 days, you can get 10% of the difference refunded.
>
> b. No. Since it is more than 14 days, you cannot get 10% of the difference re-funded.
>
> c. It depends on the cashier.
>
> d. Yes. You can get the difference refunded.

19. I bought a flat-screen TV for $500 10 days ago and found an advertisement for the same TV, at another store, on sale for $400. How much will ABC refund under this guarantee?

    a. $100
    b. $110
    c. $10
    d. $400

20. What is the purpose of this passage?

    a. To inform
    b. To educate
    c. To persuade
    d. To entertain

Questions 21 - 23 refer to the following passage.

Insects

Insects have segmented bodies supported by an exoskeleton, a hard outer covering made mostly of chitin. The segments of the body are organized into three distinctive connected units, a head, a thorax, and an abdomen. The head supports a pair of antennae, a pair of compound eyes, and three sets of appendages that form the mouthparts.

The thorax has six segmented legs and, if present in the species, two or four wings. The abdomen consists of eleven segments, though in a few species these segments may be fused together or very small.

Overall, there are 24 segments. The abdomen also contains most of the digestive, respiratory, excretory and reproductive internal structures. There is considerable variation and many adaptations in the body parts of insects especially wings, legs, antenna and mouthparts. [10]

21. How many units do insects have?

    a. Insects are divided into 24 units.

    b. Insects are divided into 3 units.

    c. Insects are divided into segments not units.

    d. It depends on the species.

22. Which of the following is true?

    a. All insects have 2 wings.

    b. All insects have 4 wings.

    c. Some insects have 2 wings.

    d. Some insects have 2 or 4 wings.

23. What is true of insect's abdomen?

    a. It contains some of the organs.

    b. It is too small for any organs.

    c. It contains all the organs.

    d. None of the above.

Questions 24 - 27 refer to the following passage.

The Daffodils
by William Wordsworth

I wandered lonely as a cloud
That floats on high o'er vales and hills,
When all at once I saw a crowd,
A host, of golden daffodils;
Beside the lake, beneath the trees,
Fluttering and dancing in the breeze.

Continuous as the stars that shine
And twinkle on the Milky Way,
They stretched in never-ending line
Along the margin of a bay:

Ten thousand saw I at a glance,
Tossing their heads in sprightly dance.

The waves beside them danced, but they
Out-did the sparkling waves in glee:
A Poet could not but be gay,
In such a jocund company:
I gazed--and gazed--but little thought
What wealth the show to me had brought:

For oft, when on my couch I lie
In vacant or in pensive mood,
They flash upon that inward eye
Which is the bliss of solitude;
And then my heart with pleasure fills,
And dances with the daffodils.

24. Is the author of this poem a lover of nature?

    a. Yes

    b. No

    c. Uncertain. There isn't enough information

25. What is the general mood of this poem?

    a. Sad

    b. Thoughtful

    c. Happy

    d. Excited

26. What does sprightly mean?

    a. Growing very fast

    b. Sad and melancholy

    c. Weak and slow

    d. Happy and full of life

27. What is jocund company?

   a. Sad
   b. Happy
   c. Joyful
   d. Boring

Questions 28 - 30 refer to the following passage.

Blood

Blood is a specialized bodily fluid that delivers nutrients and oxygen to the body's cells and transports waste products away.

In vertebrates, blood consists of blood cells suspended in a liquid called blood plasma. Plasma, which comprises 55% of blood fluid, is mostly water (90% by volume), and contains dissolved proteins, glucose, mineral ions, hormones, carbon dioxide, platelets and the blood cells themselves.

Blood cells are mainly red blood cells (also called RBCs or erythrocytes) and white blood cells, including leukocytes and platelets. Red blood cells are the most abundant cells, and contain an iron-containing protein called hemoglobin that transports oxygen through the body.

The pumping action of the heart circulates blood around the body through blood vessels. In animals with lungs, arterial blood carries oxygen from inhaled air to the tissues of the body, and venous blood carries carbon dioxide, a waste product of metabolism produced by cells, from the tissues to the lungs to be exhaled. [11]

28. What can we infer from the first paragraph in this passage?

a. Blood is responsible for transporting oxygen to the cells.

b. Blood is only red when it reaches the outside of the body.

c. Each person has about six pints of blood.

d. Blood's true function was only learned in the last century.

29. Which of these is not contained in blood plasma?

a. Hormones
b. Mineral ions
c. Calcium
d. Glucose

30. Which body part exhales carbon dioxide after venous blood has carried it from body tissues?

a. The lungs
b. The skin cells
c. The bowels
d. The sweat glands

Vocabulary

31. Choose the adjective that means shocking, terrible or wicked.

a. Pleasantries
b. Heinous
c. Shrewd
d. Provencal

32. Choose the noun that means a person of thing that tells or announces the coming of someone or something.

    a. Harbinger
    b. Evasion
    c. Bleak
    d. Craven

33. Choose a word that means the same as the underlined word.

He wasn't especially generous. All the servings were very judicious.

    a. Abundant
    b. Careful
    c. Sparing
    d. Careless

34. Because of the growing use of _____ as a fuel, corn production has greatly increased.

    a. Alcohol
    b. Ethanol
    c. Natural gas
    d. Oil

35. In heavily industrialized areas, the pollution of the air causes many to develop _____ diseases.

    a. Respiratory
    b. Cardiac
    c. Alimentary
    d. Circulatory

36. Choose the best definition of inherent.

    a. To receive money in a will
    b. An essential part of
    c. To receive money from a will
    d. None of the above

37. Choose the best vapid.

    a. adj. tasteless or bland
    b. v. To inflict, as a revenge or punishment
    c. v. to convert into gas
    d. v. to go up in smoke

38. Choose the best definition of waif.

    a. n. a sick and hungry child
    b. n. an orphan staying in a foster home
    c. n. homeless child or stray
    d. n. a type of French bread eaten with cheese

39. Choose the adjective that means similar or identical.

    a. Soluble
    b. Assembly
    c. Conclave
    d. Homologous

40. Choose a word with the same meaning as the underlined word.

We used that operating system 20 years ago, now it is obsolete.

   a. Functional
   b. Disused
   c. Obese
   d. None of the Above

41. Choose the word with the same meaning as the underlined word

His bad manners really rankle me.

   a. Annoy
   b. Obsolete
   c. Enliven
   d. None of the above

42. Because hydroelectric power is a _____ source of energy, its use is excellent for the environment.

   a. Significant
   b. Disposable
   c. Renewable
   d. Reusable

43. Choose the best definition of torpid.

   a. Fast
   b. Rapid
   c. Sluggish
   d. Violent

44. Choose the best definition of gregarious.

   a. Sociable
   b. Introverted
   c. Large
   d. Solitary

45. Choose the best definition of mutation.

   a. v. To utter with a loud and vehement voice
   b. n. change or alteration
   c. n. An act or exercise of will
   d. v. To cause to be one

46. Choose the best definition of lithe.

   a. adj. small in size
   b. adj. Artificial
   c. adj. flexible or plaint
   d. adj. fake

47. Choose the best definition of resent.

   a. adj. To express displeasure or indignation
   b. v. To cause to be one
   c. adj. Clumsy
   d. adj. strong feelings of love

48. Choose and adjective that means irrelevant or not having substance or matter

   a. Immaterial
   b. Prohibition
   c. Prediction
   d. Brokerage

49. Choose and adjective that means perfect, no faults or errors.

    a. Impeccable

    b. Formidable

    c. Genteel

    d. Disputation

50. Choose the best definition of pudgy.

    a. v. to draw general inferences

    b. Adj. fat, plump and overweight

    c. n. permanence

    d. adj. spoilt or bad condition

English Grammar, Punctuation, Capitalization and Usage.

1. Jessica's father was in the Navy, so she attended schools in <u>Newark; New Jersey, Key West; Florida, San Diego, California, and Fairbanks, Alaska.</u>

    a. Jessica's father was in the Navy, so she attended schools in Newark, New Jersey, Key West, Florida, San Diego, California, and Fairbanks, Alaska.

    b. Jessica's father was in the Navy, so she attended schools in: Newark, New Jersey, Key West, Florida, San Diego, California, and Fairbanks, Alaska.

    c. Jessica's father was in the Navy, so she attended schools in Newark, New Jersey; Key West, Florida; San Diego, California; and Fairbanks, Alaska.

    d. None of the choices are correct.

2. George wrecked John's <u>car; that was</u> the end of their friendship.

    a. George wrecked John's car that was the end of their friendship.

    b. George wrecked John's car. that was the end of their friendship.

    c. The sentence is correct.

    d. None of the choices are correct.

3. The dress was not Gina's <u>favorite, however,</u> she wore it to the dance.

    a. The dress was not Gina's favorite; however, she wore it to the dance.

    b. None of the choices are correct.

    c. The dress was not Gina's favorite, however; she wore it to the dance.

    d. The dress was not Gina's favorite however, she wore it to the dance.

4. Chris showed his dedication to golf in many <u>ways; for</u> example, he watched all the tournaments on television.

    a. Chris showed his dedication to golf in many ways, for example, he watched all the tournaments on television.

    b. The sentence is correct.

    c. Chris showed his dedication to golf in many ways, for example; he watched all the tournaments on television.

    d. Chris showed his dedication to golf in many ways for example he watched all the tournaments on television.

5. There was scarcely <u>no food</u> in the pantry, because <u>not nobody</u> ate at home.

    a. There was scarcely no food in the pantry, because nobody ate at home.

    b. There was scarcely any food in the pantry, because nobody ate at home.

    c. There was scarcely any food in the pantry, because not nobody ate at home.

    d. The sentence is correct.

6. Choose the sentence with the correct grammar.

    a. If Joe had told me the truth, I wouldn't have been so angry.
    b. If Joe would have told me the truth, I wouldn't have been so angry.
    c. I wouldn't have been so angry if Joe would have told the truth.
    d. If Joe would have telled me the truth, I wouldn't have been so angry.

7. Michael <u>have lived</u> in that house for forty years, while I <u>has owned</u> this one for only six weeks.

    a. Michael has lived in that house for forty years, while I has owned this one for only six weeks.

    b. Michael have lived in that house for forty years, while I have owned this one for only six weeks.

    c. None of the choices are correct.

    d. Michael has lived in that house for forty years, while I have owned this one for only six weeks.

8. Until you <u>take</u> the overdue books to the library, you can't <u>take</u> any new ones home.

    a. Until you take the overdue books to the library, you can't take any new ones home
    b. Until you take the overdue books to the library, you can't bring any new ones home.
    c. Until you bring the overdue books to the library, you can't take any new ones home.
    d. None of the choices are correct.

9. If they had <u>gone</u> to the party, he would have <u>gone</u> too.

    a. The sentence is correct.

    b. If they had went to the party, he would have gone too.

    c. If they had gone to the party, he would have went too.

    d. If they had went to the party, he would have went too.

10. His doctor suggested that he eat <u>fewer</u> snacks and do <u>fewer</u> lounging on the couch.

    a. His doctor suggested that he eat less snacks and do fewer lounging on the couch.

    b. His doctor suggested that he eat fewer snacks and do less lounging on the couch.

    c. His doctor suggested that he eat less snacks and do less lounging on the couch.

    d. None of the choices are correct.

11. Lee pronounced it's name incorrectly; it's an impatiens, not an impatience.

    a. The sentence is correct.

    b. Lee pronounced its name incorrectly; its an *impatiens*, not an *impatience*.

    c. Lee pronounced it's name incorrectly; its an *impatiens*, not an *impatience*.

    d. Lee pronounced its name incorrectly; it's an *impatiens*, not an *impatience*.

12. There was, however very little difference between the two.

    a. There was however, very little difference between the two.

    b. None of the choices are correct.

    c. There was; however, very little difference between the two.

    d. There was, however, very little difference between the two.

13. The Ford Motor Company was named for Henry Ford

    a. which had founded the company.

    b. who founded the company.

    c. whose had founded the company.

    d. whom had founded the company.

14. Thomas Edison _____ after he invented the light bulb, television, motion pictures, and phonograph.

    a. has always been known as the greatest inventor

    b. was always been known as the greatest inventor

    c. must have had been always known as the greatest inventor

    d. will had been known as the greatest inventor

15. The weatherman on Channel 6 said that this has been the _____.

    a. most hottest summer on record.

    b. hottest summer on record.

    c. hotter summer on record.

    d. None of the above

16. Although Joe is tall for his age, his brother Elliot is _____ of the two.

    a. the tallest

    b. more tallest

    c. the tall

    d. the taller

17. I can never remember how to use those two common words, "sell," meaning to trade a product for money, or _____ meaning an event where products are traded for less money than usual.

    a. sale-

    b. "sale,"

    c. "sale

    d. "to sale,"

18. His father is

    a. a poet and novelist

    b. poet and novelist

    c. a poet and a novelist

    d. none of the above

Practice Test Questions 2

19. The class just finished reading , _____ a short story by Carl Stephenson about a plantation owner's battle with army ants.

    a. -"Leinengen versus the Ants,"
    b. Leinengen versus the Ants,
    c. "Leinengen versus the Ants,"
    d. Leinengen versus the Ants

20. After the car was fixed it _____ again.

    a. ran good
    b. ran well
    c. would have run well
    d. ran more well

21. "Where does the sun go during the _____ asked little Kathy.

    a. night,"
    b. night?",
    c. night,?"
    d. night?"

22. Vegetables are a <u>healthy</u> food; eating them can make you more <u>healthy</u>.

    a. Vegetables are a healthy food; eating them can make you more healthful.
    b. Vegetables are a healthful food; eating them can make you more healthful.
    c. None of the choices are correct.
    d. Vegetables are a healthful food; eating them can make you more healthy.

23. When James went <u>in</u> his room, he found that his clothes had been put <u>in</u> the closet.

>a. When James went into his room, he found that his clothes had been put in the closet.
>
>b. None of the choices are correct.
>
>c. When James went into his room, he found that his clothes had been put into the closet.
>
>d. When James went in his room, he found that his clothes had been put into the closet.

24. After you lay the books on the counter, you may lay down for a nap.

>a. The sentence is correct.
>
>b. After you lie the books on the counter, you may lay down for a nap.
>
>c. After you lay the books on the counter, you may lie down for a nap.
>
>d. After you lay the books on the counter, you may lay down for a nap.

25. Don <u>would never of thought</u> of that book, but you <u>could have reminded</u> him.

>a. Don would never have thought of that book, but you could have reminded him.
>
>b. None of the choices are correct.
>
>c. Don would never have thought of that book, but you could of have reminded him.
>
>d. Don would never of thought of that book, but you could of reminded him.

26. Mrs. Foster <u>learned</u> me many things, but I was <u>taught</u> the most by Mr. Wallace.

    a. Mrs. Foster taught me many things, but I learned the most from Mr. Wallace.

    b. The sentence is correct.

    c. Mrs. Foster learned me many things, but I learned the most from Mr. Wallace.

    d. None of the choices are correct.

27. He did not have to <u>loose</u> the race; if only his shoes weren't so <u>loose</u>!

    a. He did not have to loose the race; if only his shoes weren't so lose!

    b. He did not have to lose the race; if only his shoes weren't so loose!

    c. The sentence is correct.

    d. None of the choices are correct.

28. The attorney did not want to <u>prosecute</u> the defendant; his goal was to <u>prosecute</u> the guilty party.

    a. None of the choices are correct.

    b. The attorney did not want to persecute the defendant; his goal was to persecute the guilty party.

    c. The attorney did not want to prosecute the defendant; his goal was to persecute the guilty party.

    d. The attorney did not want to persecute the defendant; his goal was to prosecute the guilty party.

29. The speeches must <u>proceed</u> the election; the election cannot <u>proceed</u> without hearing from the candidates.

    a. The speeches must precede the election; the election cannot proceed without hearing from the candidates.

    b. The speeches must precede the election; the election cannot precede without hearing from the candidates.

    c. The speeches must proceed the election; the election cannot precede without hearing from the candidates.

    d. The sentence is correct.

30. My best friend said, "Always Count your Change."

    a. My best friend said, "always count your change."

    b. The sentence is correct.

    c. My best friend said, "Always count your change."

    d. None of the choices are correct.

31. The <u>Victorian Era</u> was in the <u>nineteenth century</u>.

    a. The sentence is correct.

    b. The victorian era was in the nineteenth century.

    c. The Victorian Era was in the Nineteenth century.

    d. The Victorian era was in the Nineteenth century.

32. I prefer <u>pepsi</u> to <u>Coke</u>.

    a. I prefer pepsi to coke.

    b. The sentence is correct.

    c. I prefer Pepsi to Coke.

    d. None of the choices are correct.

33. I always have <u>french fries</u> with my <u>coke</u>.

    a. The sentence is correct.
    b. I always have french fries with my Coke.
    c. I always have French Fries with my Coke.
    d. None of the choices are correct.

34. The <u>blue Jays</u> are my favorite team.

    a. The blue jays are my favorite team.
    b. The sentence is correct.
    c. The Blue Jays are my favorite team.
    d. None of the choices are correct.

35. The <u>Southwest</u> is the best part of the country.

    a. The sentence is correct.
    b. The southwest is the best part of the country.
    c. The southwest is the best part of the Country.
    d. None of the choices are correct.

Mathematics

1. Translate the following into an equation:

2 plus a number divided by 7.

    a. $(2 + X)/7$
    b. $(7 + X)/2$
    c. $(2 + 7)/X$
    d. $2/(7 + X)$

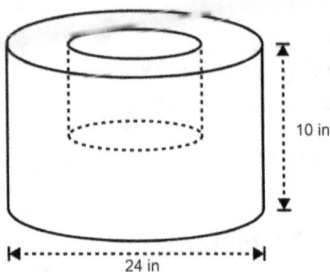

Note: figure not drawn to scale

2. What is the volume of the above solid made by a hollow cylinder that is half the size (in all dimensions) of the larger cylinder?

 a. 1440 π in³
 b. 1260 π in³
 c. 1040 π in³
 d. 960 π in³

3. If a train travels at 72 kilometers per hour, how far will it travel in 12 seconds?

 a. 200 m
 b. 220 m
 c. 240 m
 d. 260 m

4. Tony bought 15 dozen eggs for $80. 16 eggs were broken during loading and unloading. He sold the remaining eggs for $0.54 each. What will be his percent profit?

 a. 11%
 b. 11.2%
 c. 11.5%
 d. 12%

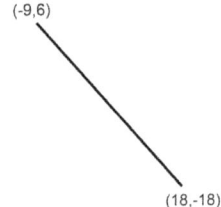

5. What is the slope of the line above?

   a. -8/9
   b. 9/8
   c. -9/8
   d. 8/9

6. In a class of 83 students, 72 are present. What percent of students are absent?

   a. 12%
   b. 13%
   c. 14%
   d. 15%

7. $9ab^2 + 8ab^2 =$

   a. ab^2
   b. $17ab^2$
   c. 17
   d. $17a^2b^2$

8. The total expense of building a fence around a square shaped field is $2000 at a rate of $5 per meter. What is the length of one side?

   a. 80 meters
   b. 100 meters
   c. 40 meters
   d. 320 meters

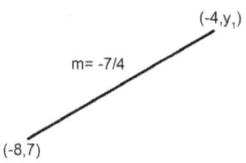

9. With the data given above, what is the value of y_1?

   a. 0
   b. -7
   c. 7
   d. 8

10. In a local election at polling station A, 945 voters cast their vote out of 1270 registered voters. At polling station B, 860 cast their vote out of 1050 registered voters and at station C, 1210 cast their vote out of 1440 registered voters. What was the total turnout including all three polling stations?

   a. 70%
   b. 74%
   c. 76%
   d. 80%

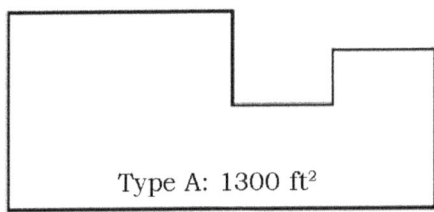

Type A: 1300 ft²

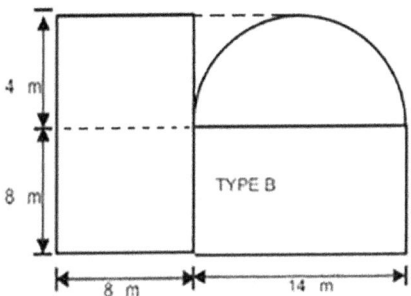

Note: Figure not drawn to scale

11. The price of houses in a certain subdivision is based on the total area. Susan is watching her budget and wants to choose the house with the lowest area. Which house type, A (1300 ft2) or B, should she choose if she would like the house with the lowest price? (1 m2 = 10.76 ft2 & π = 22/7)

   a. Type B is smaller at 140 ft²
   b. Type A is smaller
   c. Type B is smaller at 855 ft²
   d. Type B is larger

Consider the following graph.

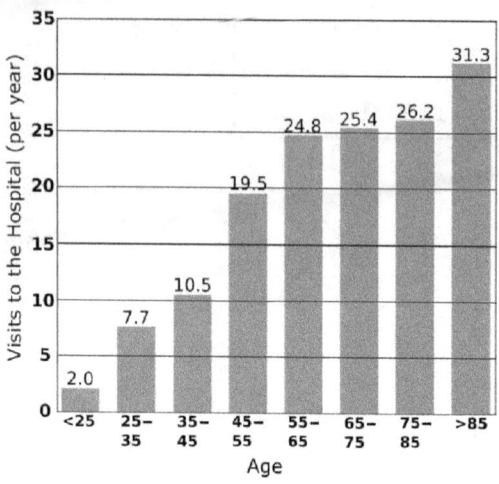

12. How many hospital visits per year does a person aged 85 or more make?

    a. 26.2

    b. 31.3

    c. More than 31.3

    d. A decision cannot be made from this graph.

13. Based on this graph, how many visits per year do you expect a person that is 95 or older to make?

    a. More than 31.3

    b. Less than 31.3

    c. 31.3

    d. A decision cannot be made from this graph.

14. How much water can be stored in a cylindrical container 5 meters in diameter and 12 meters high?

Note: figure not drawn to scale

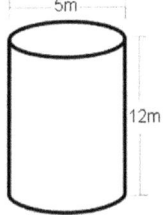

a. 235.65 m³
b. 223.65 m³
c. 240.65 m³
d. 252.65 m³

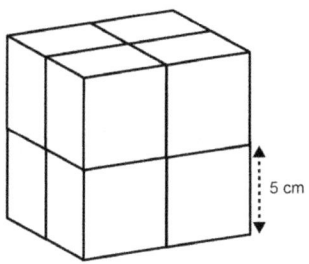

Note: figure not drawn to scale

15. Assuming the figure above is composed of cubes, what is the volume?

a. 125 cm³
b. 875 cm³
c. 1000 cm³
d. 500 cm³

16. Choose the expression the figure represents.

    a. X > 2
    b. X ≥ 2
    c. X < 2
    d. X ≤ 2

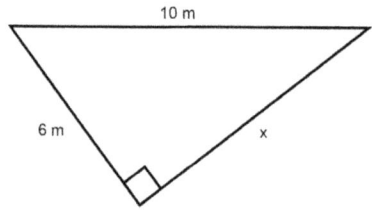

Note: figure not drawn to scale

17. What is the length of the missing side in the triangle above?

    a. 6
    b. 4
    c. 8
    d. 5

18. 60 is 75% of x. Solve for x.

    a. 80
    b. 90
    c. 75
    d. 70

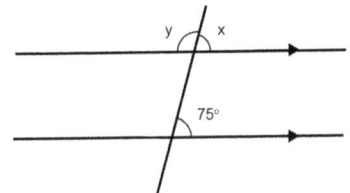

19. What is the value of the angle y?

    a. 25°
    b. 15°
    c. 30°
    d. 105°

20. Express 71/1000 as a decimal.

    a. .71
    b. .0071
    c. .071
    d. 7.1

21. .33 × .59 =

    a. .1947
    b. 1.947
    c. .0197
    d. .1817

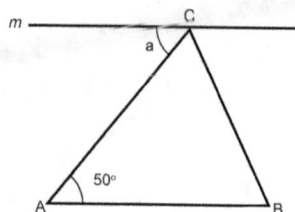

Note: Figure not drawn to scale

22. If the line *m* is parallel to the side AB of △ABC, what is angle *a*?

    a. 130°
    b. 25°
    c. 65°
    d. 50°

23. 7x − 9 = 47. Solve for x.

    a. 8
    b. 7
    c. 9
    d. 6

24. What number is in the ten thousandths place in 1.7389

    a. 1
    b. 8
    c. 9
    d. 3

25. .87 - .48 =

a. .39
b. .49
c. .41
d. .37

26. Which is the equivalent decimal number for forty nine thousandths?

a. .49
b. .0049
c. .049
d. 4.9

27. Which of the following is not a fraction equivalent to 3/4?

a. 6/8
b. 9/12
c. 12/18
d. 21/28

28. Which one of the following is greater than a third?

a. 84/231
b. 6/35
c. 3/22
d. b and c

29. Which of the following numbers is the greatest?

   a. 1
   b. $\sqrt{2}$
   c. 3/2
   d. 4/3

30. $2b + 9b - 5b = 0$

   a. 3b
   b. 6b
   c. 4b
   d. 8b

31. $(4Y^3 - 2Y^2) + (7Y^2 + 3y - y) =$

   a. $4y^3 + 9y^2 + 4y$
   b. $5y^3 + 5y^2 + 3y$
   c. $4y^3 + 7y^2 + 2y$
   d. $4y^3 + 5y^2 + 2y$

32. $4.7 + .9 + .01 =$

   a. 5.5
   b. 6.51
   c. 5.61
   d. 5.7

33. $7(2y + 8) + 1 - 4(y + 5) =$

   a. $10y + 36$
   b. $10y + 77$
   c. $18y + 37$
   d. $10y + 37$

(18,12)

(9,-6)

34. What is the distance between the two points?

    a. ≈19
    b. 20
    c. ≈21
    d. ≈22

35. 60% of x is 12. Solve for x.

    a. 18
    b. 15
    c. 25
    d. 20

36. .84 ÷ .7 =

    a. .12
    b. 12
    c. .012
    d. 1.2

37. 6(x − 4) = 3x + 12. Solve for x.

    a. 15
    b. 8
    c. 12
    d. 14

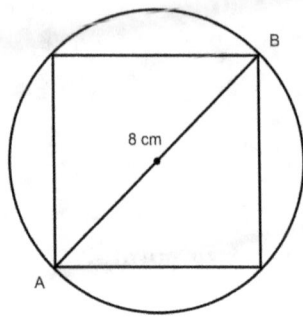

Note: figure not drawn to scale

38. What is area of the circle?

    a. 4 π cm²
    b. 12 π cm²
    c. 10 π cm²
    d. 16 π cm²

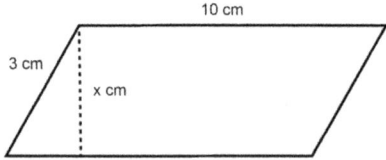

Note: figure not drawn to scale

39. What is the perimeter of the parallelogram above?

    a. 12 cm
    b. 26 cm
    c. 13 cm
    d. (13+x) cm

40. Richard gives 's' amount of salary to each of his 'n' employees weekly. If he has 'x' amount of money then how many days he can employ these 'n' employees.

    a. sx/7n
    b. 7x/nx
    c. nx/7s
    d. 7x/ns

41. Express 87% as a decimal.

    a. .087
    b. 8.7
    c. .87
    d. 87

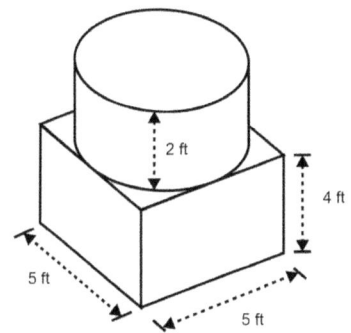

Note: figure not drawn to scale

42. What is the approximate total volume of the above solid?

    a. 120 ft³
    b. 100 ft³
    c. 140 ft³
    d. 160 ft³

43. Susan wants to buy a leather jacket that costs $545.00 and is on sale for 10% off. What is the approximate cost?

    a. $525
    b. $450
    c. $475
    d. $500

44. Translate the following into an equation:

Five greater than 3 times a number.

    a. 3X + 5
    b. 5X + 3
    c. (5 + 3)X
    d. 5(3 + X)

45. What is the slope of the line above?

    a. 1
    b. 2
    c. 3
    d. -2

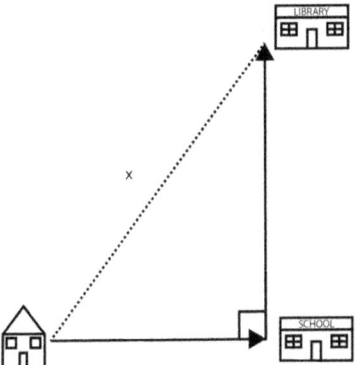

Note: figure not drawn to scale

46. Every day starting from his home Peter travels due east 3 kilometers to the school. After school he travels due north 4 kilometers to the library. What is the distance between Peter's home and the library?

    a. 15 km
    b. 10 km
    c. 5 km
    d. 12 ½ km

47. The cost of waterproofing canvas is .50 per square yard. What is the total cost for waterproofing a canvas truck cover that is 15' x 24'?

    a. $18.00
    b. $6.67
    c. $180.00
    d. $20.00

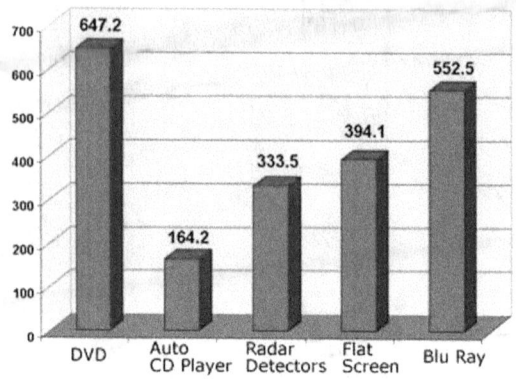

48. Consider the graph above. What is the third best-selling product?

    a. Radar Detectors
    b. Flat Screen TV
    c. Blu Ray
    d. Auto CD Players

49. Which two products are the closest in the number of sales?

    a. Blu Ray and Flat Screen TV
    b. Flat Screen TV and Radar Detectors
    c. Radar Detectors and Auto CD Players
    d. DVD players and Blu Ray

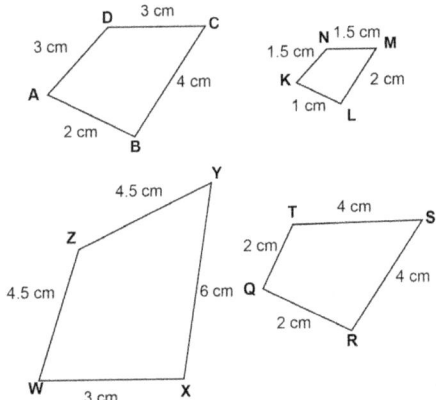

50. Which of the above quadrilaterals are similar?

    a. All are similar
    b. QRST, KLMN, WXYZ
    c. ABCD, KLMN, WXYZ
    d. None of the choices are correct.

Answer Key

Reading Comprehension

1. B
We can infer an important part of the respiratory system are the lungs. From the passage, "Molecules of oxygen and carbon dioxide are passively exchanged, by diffusion, between the gaseous external environment and the blood. This exchange process occurs in the alveolar region of the lungs."

Therefore, one primary function for the respiratory system is the exchange of oxygen and carbon dioxide, and this process occurs in the lungs. We can therefore infer that the lungs are an important part of the respiratory system.

2. C
The process by which molecules of oxygen and carbon dioxide are passively exchanged is diffusion.

This is a definition type question. Scan the passage for references to "oxygen," "carbon dioxide," or "exchanged."

3. A
The organ that plays an important role in gas exchange in amphibians is the skin.

Scan the passage for references to "amphibians," and find the answer.

4. A
The three physiological zones of the respiratory system are Conducting, transitional, respiratory zones.

5. B
This warranty does not cover a product that you have tried to fix yourself. From paragraph two, "This limited warranty does not cover … any unauthorized disassembly, repair, or modification. "

6. C
ABC Electric could either replace or repair the fan, provided the other conditions are met. ABC Electric has the option to

repair or replace.

7. B
The warranty does not cover a stove damaged in a flood. From the passage, "This limited warranty does not cover any damage to the product from improper installation, accident, abuse, misuse, natural disaster, insufficient or excessive electrical supply, abnormal mechanical or environmental conditions."

A flood is an "abnormal environmental condition," and a natural disaster, so it is not covered.

8. A
A missing part is an example of defective workmanship. This is an error made in the manufacturing process. A defective part is not considered workmanship.

9. A
Low blood sugar occurs both in diabetics and healthy adults.

10. B
None of the statements are the author's opinion.

11. A
The author's purpose is the inform.

12. A
The only statement that is not a detail is, "A doctor can diagnosis this medical condition by asking the patient questions and testing."

13. A
Based on the partial table of contents, this book is most likely about how to answer multiple choice.

14. B
This passage describes the different categories for traditional stories. The other choices are facts from the passage, not the main idea of the passage. The main idea of a passage will always be the most general statement. For example, choice A, Myths, fables, and folktales are not the same thing, and

each describes a specific type of story. This is a true statement from the passage, but not the main idea of the passage, since the passage also talks about how some cultures may classify a story as a myth and others as a folktale.

The statement, from choice B, Traditional stories can be categorized in different ways by different people, is a more general statement that describes the passage.

15. B
Choice B is the best choice, categories that group traditional stories according to certain characteristics.

Choices A and C are false and can be eliminated right away. Choice D is designed to confuse. Choice D may be true, but it is not mentioned in the passage.

16. D
The best answer is choice D, traditional stories themselves are a part of the larger category of folklore, which may also include costumes, gestures, and music.

All the other choices are false. Traditional stories are part of the larger category of Folklore, which includes other things, not the other way around.

17. A
There is a distinct difference between a myth and a legend, although both are folktales.

18. B
The time limit for radar detectors is 14 days. Since you made the purchase 15 days ago, you do not qualify for the guarantee.

19. B
Since you made the purchase 10 days ago, you are covered by the guarantee. Since it is an advertised price at a different store, ABC Electric will "beat" the price by 10% of the difference, which is,

500 – 400 = 100 – difference in price

100 X 10% = $10 – 10% of the difference

The advertised lower price is $400. ABC will beat this price by 10% so they will refund $100 + 10 = $110.

20. C
The purpose of this passage is to persuade.

21. B
From the first paragraph, "The segments of the body are organized into three distinctive connected units, a head, a thorax, and an abdomen."

This question tries to confuse 'segments' and 'units.'

22. D
This question tries to confuse. Read the passage carefully to find reference to the number of wings. "…if present in the species, two or four wings."

From this, we can conclude some insects have no wings, (if present …) some have 2 wings and some have 4 wings.

23. A
The question asks about the abdomen and choices refer to organs in the abdomen. The passage says, "The abdomen also contains most of the digestive, respiratory, … "

The choices are,

       a. It contains some of the organs.

       b. It is too small for any organs.

       c. It contains all the organs.

       d. None of the above.

Choice A is true, but we need to see if there is better choice before answering. Choice B is not true. Choice C is not true since the relevant sentence says 'most' not 'all.' Choice D can be eliminated since choice A is true.

Given there is not better choice, choice A is the best answer.

24. A
The author is enjoying the daffodils very much and so we can infer that he is a lover of nature.

25. C
The mood of this poem is happy. From the last line,

And then my heart with pleasure fills,
And dances with the daffodils.

26. D
Sprightly means happy and full of life. From the lines before and after sprightly, we can see it means happy.

Ten thousand saw I at a glance,
Tossing their heads in sprightly dance.

The waves beside them danced, but they
Out-did the sparkling waves in glee:

27. C
Joyful is the best answer. Happy is a possible answer, but joyful is better. Jocund means jovial, exuberant, light-hearted; merry and in high spirits. From the poem,

Ten thousand saw I at a glance,
Tossing their heads in sprightly dance.

The waves beside them danced, but they
Out-did the sparkling waves in glee:

28. A
We can infer that blood is responsible for transporting oxygen to the cells.

29. C
Calcium is not contained in blood plasma.

From the passage, "[Blood Plasma] contains dissolved proteins, glucose, mineral ions, hormones, carbon dioxide, platelets and the blood cells themselves."

30. A
The lungs exhale the carbon dioxide after venous blood has been carried from body tissues.

31. B
Heinous: adj. shocking, terrible or wicked.

32. A
Harbinger: n. a person of thing that tells or announces the coming of someone or something

33. B
Judicious: Having, or characterized by, good judgment or sound thinking.

34. B
Ethanol: n. a colorless volatile flammable liquid C_2H_6O.

35. A
Respiratory: adj. Of, relating to, or affecting respiration or the organs of respiration.

36. B
Inherent: Naturally a part or consequence of something.

37. A
Vapid: adj. tasteless or bland.

38. C
Waif: n. homeless child or stray.

39. D
Homologous: adj. similar or identical.

40. B
Obsolete: adj. no longer in use; gone into disuse; disused or neglected.

41. A
Rankle: v. To cause irritation or deep bitterness.

42. D
Reusable

43. C
Torpid: adj. Lazy, lethargic or apathetic.

44. A
Gregarious: adj. Describing one who enjoys being in crowds and socializing.

45. B
Mutation: n. a change or alteration.

46. C
Lithe: adj. flexible or pliant.

47. A
Resent: v. to express displeasure or indignation.

48. A
Immaterial: irrelevant not having substance or matter.

49. A
Impeccable: adj. perfect, no faults or errors.

50. B
Pudgy: adj. fat, plump or overweight.

English

1. C
The semicolon is used in a list where the list items have internal punctuation, such as "Key West, Florida."

2. C
The semicolon links independent clauses. An independent clause can form a complete sentence by itself.

3. A
The semicolon links independent clauses with a conjunction (However).

4. B
The sentence is correct. The semicolon links independent clauses. An independent clause can form a complete sentence by itself.

5. B
Double negative sentence. In double negative sentences, one negatives is replaced with "any."

6. A
The third conditional is used for talking about an unreal situation (that did not happen) in the past. For example, "If I had studied harder, [if clause] I would have passed the exam [main clause]. Which is the same as, "I failed the exam, because I didn't study hard enough."

7. D
Present perfect. You cannot use the Present Perfect with specific time expressions such as: yesterday, one year ago, last week, when I was a child, at that moment, that day, one day, etc. The Present Perfect is used with unspecific expressions such as: ever, never, once, many times, several times, before, so far, already, yet, etc.

8. C
Bring vs. Take. Usage depends on your location. Something coming your way is brought to you. Something going away is taken from you.

9. A
The sentence is correct. Went vs. Gone. Went is the simple past tense. Gone is used in the past perfect.

10. B
Fewer vs. Less. 'Fewer' is used with countables and 'less' is used with uncountables.

11. D
Its vs. It's. 'It's' is a contraction for it is or it has. 'Its' is a possessive pronoun meaning, more or less, of 'it,' or belonging to 'it.'

12. D
When using 'however,' place a comma before and after.

13. B
"Who" is the best choice because the sentence refers to a person.

14. A
Past perfect is the correct form because it refers to something that happened in the past (he was the greatest inventor) and is still true today.

15. C
The superlative "hottest" is used when expressing the highest degree, or a degree greater than that of anything it is compared with.

16. D
When comparing two, use 'the taller.' When comparing more than two, use 'the tallest.'

17. B
Here the word "sale" is used as a "word" and not as a word in the sentence, so quotation marks are used.

18. C
His father is a poet and a novelist. It is necessary to use 'a' twice in this sentence for the two distinct things.

19. C
Titles of short stories are enclosed in quotation marks, and commas always go inside quotation marks.

20. B
Present tense, "ran well" is correct. "Ran good" is never correct.

21. D
Punctuation always goes inside quotation marks.

22. D
Healthful vs. Healthy. 'Healthy' is used to describe something that is of good for your health and 'healthful' refers to habits or types.

23. A
In vs. Into. 'In' a room means inside. 'Into' refers to movement or action.

24. C
Lay vs. Lie. Lie requires an object and lay does not. So you can lie down, (no object. and you lay a book on the floor.

25. A
The third conditional is used for talking about an unreal situation (that did not happen) in the past. For example, "If I had studied harder, [if clause] I would have passed the exam [main clause]. Which is the same as, "I failed the exam, because I didn't study hard enough."

26. A
Learn vs. Teach. Learning is what students do, and teaching is what teachers do.

27. B
Lose vs. Loose. Lose is to no longer have, or to lose a race. Loose is not tied or able to move freely.

28. D
Persecute vs. Prosecute. To prosecute is to have a legal claim against someone and to persecute is to harass.

29. A
Precede vs. Proceed. To precede is to go first or in front of. To proceed is to go forward.

30. A
Quoted speech is not capitalized.

31. A
The sentence is correct. Periods and events are capitalized but not century numbers.

32. C
Brand names are capitalized.

33. B
Generic terms such as 'french fries' are not capitalized. Brand names are capitalized.

34. C
The names of sports teams, as proper nouns, are capitalized. In this sentence, the full name is capitalized, Blue Jays.

35. A
The sentence is correct. North, South, East, and West when used as sections of the country, but not as compass directions.

Mathematics

1. A
2 + a number divided by 7.
(2 + X) divided by 7.
(2 + X)/7

2. B
Total Volume = Volume of large cylinder - Volume of small cylinder

Volume of a cylinder = area of base • height = $\pi r^2 \cdot h$

Total Volume = $(\pi \cdot 12^2 \cdot 10) - (\pi \cdot 6^2 \cdot 5) = 1440\pi - 180\pi$

= 1260π in^3

3. C
1 hour is equal to 3,600 seconds and 1 kilometer is equal to 1000 meters.

Since this train travels 72 kilometers per hour, this means that it covers 72,000 meters in 3,600 seconds.

If it travels 72,000 meters in 3,600 seconds

It travels x meters in 12 seconds

By cross multiplication: x = 72,000 • 12 / 3,600

x = 240 meters

4. A
Let us first mention the money Tony spent: $80

Now we need to find the money Tony earned:

He had 15 dozen eggs = 15•12 = 180 eggs. 16 eggs were broken. So,

Remaining number of eggs that Tony sold = 180 – 16 = 164.

Total amount he earned for selling 164 eggs = 164•0.54 = $88.56.

As a summary, he spent $80 and earned $88.56.

The profit is the difference: 88.56 - 80 = $8.56

Percentage profit is found by proportioning the profit to the money he spent:

8.56•100/80 = 10.7%

Checking the answers, we round 10.7 to the nearest whole number: 11%

5. A
If we know the coordinates of two points on a line, we can find the slope (m) with the below formula:

$m = (y_2 - y_1)/(x_2 - x_1)$ where (x_1, y_1) represent the coordinates of one point and (x_2, y_2) the other.

In this question:

$(-9, 6) : x_1 = -9, y_1 = 6$

$(18, -18) : x_2 = 18, y_2 = -18$

Inserting these values into the formula:

$m = (-18 - 6)/(18 - (-9)) = (-24)/(27)$ ... Simplifying by 3:

$m = -8/9$

6. B
Number of absent students = 83 – 72 = 11

Percentage of absent students is found by proportioning the number of absent students to total number of students in the class = 11•100/83 = 13.25

Checking the answers, we round 13.25 to the nearest whole number: 13%

7. B

$ab^2 (9+8) = 17ab^2$

8. B

Total expense is $2000 and we are informed that $5 is spent per meter. Combining these two information, we know that the total length of the fence is 2000/5 = 400 meters.

The fence is built around a square-shaped field. If one side of the square is "a," the perimeter of the square is "4a." Here, the perimeter is equal to 400 meters. So,

400 = 4a

100 = a → this means that one side of the square is equal to 100 meters

9. A

If we know the coordinates of two points on a line, we can find the slope (m) with the below formula:
$m = (y_2 - y_1)/(x_2 - x_1)$ where (x_1, y_1) represent the coordinates of one point and (x_2, y_2) the other.

In this question:

$(-4, y_1) : x_1 = -4, y_1 =$ we will find

$(-8, 7) : x_2 = -8, y_2 = 7$

m = -7/4

Inserting these values into the formula:

$-7/4 = (7 - y_1)/(-8 - (-4))$

$-7/4 = (7 - y_1)/(-8 + 4)$

$7/(-4) = (7 - y_1)/(-4)$ ... Simplifying the denominators of both sides by -4:

$7 = 7 - y_1$

$0 = -y_1$

$y_1 = 0$

10. D

To find the total turnout in all three polling stations, we need

to proportion the number of voters to the number of all registered voters.
Number of total voters = 945 + 860 + 1210 = 3015

Number of total registered voters = 1270 + 1050 + 1440 = 3760

Percentage turnout over all three polling stations = 3015•100/3760 = 80.19%

Checking the answers, we round 80.19 to the nearest whole number: 80%

11. D
Area of Type B consists of two rectangles and a half circle. We can find these three areas and sum them up to find the total area:

Area of the left rectangle: (4 + 8)•8 = 96 m^2

Area of the right rectangle: 14•8 = 112 m^2

The diameter of the circle is equal to 14 m. So, the radius is 14/2 = 7:

Area of the half circle = (1/2)•πr^2 = (1/2)•(22/7)•(7)^2 = (1•22•49)/(2•7) = 77 m^2

Area of Type B = 96 + 112 + 77 = 285 m^2

Converting this area to ft^2: 285 m^2 = 285•10.76 ft^2 = 3066.6 ft^2

Type B is (3066.6 - 1300 = 1766.6 ft^2) 1766.6 ft^2 larger than type A.

12. B
Based on this graph, a person that is 85 will make 31.3 visits to the hospital every year.

13. A
Based on this graph, the number of visits per year is going up as age goes up, so we can expect a person that is 95 to have more than 31.3 visits to the hospital each year.

14. A

The formula of the volume of cylinder is the base area multiplied by the height. As the formula:

Volume of a cylinder = $\pi r^2 h$. Where π is 3.142, r is radius of the cross sectional area, and h is the height.

We know that the diameter is 5 meters, so the radius is 5/2 = 2.5 meters.

The volume is: V = $3.142 \cdot 2.5^2 \cdot 12$ = 235.65 m³.

15. C

The large cube is made up of 8 smaller cubes with 5 cm sides. The volume of a cube is found by the third power of the length of one side.

Volume of the large cube = Volume of the small cube•8

= $(5^3) \cdot 8$ = 125•8

= 1000 cm³

There is another solution for this question. Find the side length of the large cube. There are two cubes rows with 5 cm length for each. So, one side of the large cube is 10 cm.

The volume of this large cube is equal to 10^3 = 1000 cm³

16. A

The line is pointing towards numbers greater than 2. The equation is therefore, X > 2.

17. C

Pythagorean Theorem:
$(Hypotenuse)^2 = (Perpendicular)^2 + (Base)^2$
$h^2 = a^2 + b^2$

Given: a = 6, h = 10
$h^2 = a^2 + b^2$
$b^2 = h^2 - a^2$
$b^2 = 10^2 + 6^2$
$b^2 = 100 - 36$
$b^2 = 64$
$b = 8$

18. A
60/x = 75/100
60* 100/X = 75
6000/75 = X
X = 80

19. D
Two parallel lines intersected by a third line with angles of 75°
x = 75° (corresponding angles)
x + y = 180° (supplementary angles)
y = 180° - 75°
y = 105°

20. C
71 ÷ 1000 = 0.071.

21. A
.33 × .59 = .1947

22. D
Two parallel lines (m & side AB) intersected by side AC. This means that 50° and a angles are interior angles. So:
a = 50° (interior angles).

23. A
Collect like terms, 7x = 47 + 9 = 56,
divide both sides by 7
x = 8

24. C
The ten thousandths place in 1.7389 will be the 4th decimal place, 9.

25. A
.87 - .48 = 0.39.

26. C
Forty nine thousandths will place the '9' in the 3rd decimal place, 0.049.

27. C
a. 3/4 * 2/2 = 6/8
b. 3/4 * 3/3 = 9/12
c. 3/4 * 4/4 = 12/18 – Incorrect!

28. A
    a. 84/231 = 12/33 > 1/3
    b. 6/35 = 1/5 < 1/3
    c. 3/22 = 1/7 < 1/3

29. C
Here are the choices:
a. 1
b. $\sqrt{2} = 1.414$
c. 3/2 = 1.5   Largest number
d. 4/3 = 1.33

30. B
Collecting similar terms (algebraic addition).
2b + 9b – 5b = 11b - 5b = 6b

31. D
Remove parenthesis
$4Y^3 - 2Y^2 + 7Y^2 + 3Y - Y$
add and subtract like terms, $4Y^3 + 5Y^2 + 2Y$

32. C
4.7 + .9 + .01 = 5.61.

33. D
Open parenthesis, (7 x 2y + 7 x 8) + 1- (4 x y -20) =
14y + 56 + 1 - 4y - 20,
Collect like terms =14y -4y + 56 + 1 – 20 = 10y + 37

34. D
The distance between two points is found by
= $[(x_2 - x_1)^2+(y_2 - y_1)^2]^{1/2}$

In this question:

(18, 12) : $x_1 = 18$, $y_1 = 12$

(9, -6) : $x_2 = 9$, $y_2 = -6$

Distance $= [(9 - 18)^2 + (-6 - 12)^2]^{1/2}$

$= [(-9)^2 + (-18)^2]^{1/2}$

$= (9^2 + 2^2 \cdot 9^2)^{1/2}$

$= (9^2(1 + 5))^{1/2}$ ... We can take 9 out of the square root:

$= 9 \cdot 6^{1/2}$

$= 9\sqrt{6}$

$= 9 \cdot 2.45$

$= 22.04$

The distance is approximately 22 units.

35. D
60% of x = 12

(60/100)x = 12

60x = 1200

x = 20

36. D
.84/.7 = 1.2

37. C
6x - 24 = 3x + 12
6x - 3x = 12 + 24
3x = 36
x = 12

38. D
We have a circle given with diameter 8 cm and a square located within the circle. We are asked to find the area of the circle for which we only need to know the length of the radius that is the half of the diameter.
Area of circle $= \pi r^2$ ... r = 8/2 = 4 cm

Area of circle $= \pi * 4^2$

$= 16\pi$ cm² ... As we notice, the inner square has no role in this question.

39. B
Perimeter of a parallelogram is the sum of the sides.
Perimeter = 2(l + b)
Perimeter = 2(3 +10), 2 x 13
Perimeter = 26 cm.

40. D
He pays 'ns' amount to the employees for 7 days. The 'x' amount will be for '7x/ns' days.

41. C
Converting a percentage to a decimal – divide the numerator by the denominator.
87 ÷ 100 = 0.87.

42. C
Volume of a cylinder is $\pi \times r^2 \times h$
Diameter = 5 ft. so radius is 2.5 ft.
Volume of cylinder= $\pi \times 2.5^2 \times 2$
= $\pi \times 6.25 \times 2 = 12.5 \pi$
Approximate π to 3.142
Volume of the cylinder = 39.25

Volume of a rectangle = height X width X length.
= 5 X 5 X 4 = 100

Total volume = Volume of rectangular solid + volume of cylinder
Total volume = 100 + 39.25
Total volume = 139.25 ft^3 or about 140 ft^3

43. D
The jacket costs $545.00 so we can round up to $550. 10% of $550 is 55. We can round down to $50, which is easier to work with. $550 - $50 is $500. The jacket will cost about $500.

The actual cost will be 10% X 545 = $54.50
545 – 54.50 = $490.50

44. A
Five greater than 3 times a number.
5 + 3 times a number.
5 + 3X

45. B

If we know the coordinates of two points on a line, we can find the slope (m) with the below formula:
m = $(y_2 - y_1)/(x_2 - x_1)$ where (x_1, y_1) represent the coordinates of one point and (x_2, y_2) the other.

In this question:

$(-4, -4) : x_1 = -4, y_1 = -4$

$(-1, 2) : x_2 = -1, y_2 = 2$

Inserting these values into the formula:

m = $(2 - (-4))/(-1 - (-4)) = (2 + 4)/(-1 + 4) = 6/3$ ... Simplifying by 3:

m = 2

46. C
Pythagorean Theorem:
(Hypotenuse)² = (Perpendicular)² + (Base)²
$h^2 = a^2 + b^2$

Given: $3^2 + 4^2 = h^2$
$h^2 = 9 + 16$
h = $\sqrt{25}$
h = 5

47. D
First calculate total square feet, which is 15 X 24 = 360 sq. ft. Next convert to square yards, (1sq. ft. = 0.1111 sq. yards) which is 360 X 0.1111 = 39.9999 or 40 square yards. At $0.50 per square yard, the total cost is $20.

48. B
Flat Screen TVs are the third best-selling product.

49. B
The two products that are closest in the number of sales, are Flat Screen TVs and Radar Detectors.

50. C
Comparing respective sides, ABCD, KLMN, WXYZ are similar.

Conclusion

CONGRATULATIONS! You have made it this far because you have applied yourself diligently to practicing for the exam and no doubt improved your potential score considerably! Getting into a good school is a huge step in a journey that might be challenging at times but will be many times more rewarding and fulfilling. That is why being prepared is so important.

Study then Practice and then Succeed!

Good Luck!

FREE Ebook Version

Download a FREE Ebook version of the publication!

Suitable for tablets, iPad, iPhone, or any smart phone.

Go to
http://tinyurl.com/n5ks7e3

CHSPE Test Strategy!

Learn to increase your score using time-tested secrets for answering multiple choice questions!

This practice book has everything you need to know about answering multiple choice questions on the CHSPE!

You will learn 12 strategies for answering multiple choice questions and then practice each strategy with over 45 reading comprehension multiple choice questions, with extensive commentary from exam experts!

Also included are strategies and practice questions for basic math, plus math tips, tricks and shortcuts!

Maybe you have read this kind of thing before, and maybe feel you don't need it, and you are not sure if you are going to buy this Book.

Remember though, it only a few percentage points divide the PASS from the FAIL students.

Even if our multiple choice strategies increase your score by a few percentage points, isn't that worth it?

https://www.createspace.com/4120179

Enter Code LYFZGQB5 for 25% off!

Get Organized, Study Less and Get Higher Marks!

Here is what you will learn:

- How to Organize your Study Space

- Four different strategies for taking notes - Taking notes is a critical skill for success. Sample lectures with example notes in 4 different styles, with complete explanation and exercises.

- Reading strategies for textbooks, essays, novels and literature

- How to Concentrate - What is concentration and how do you do it!

- Using Flash Cards - Complete guide to using flash cards including the Leitner method.

and LOT more... Including time management, sleep, nutrition, motivation, brain food, procrastination, study schedules and more!

https://www.createspace.com/4060298

Enter Code LYFZGQB5 for 25% off!

Endnotes

Reading Comprehension passages where noted below are used under the Creative Commons Attribution-ShareAlike 3.0 License

http://en.wikipedia.org/wiki/Wikipedia:Text_of_Creative_Commons_Attribution-ShareAlike_3.0_Unported_License

[1] Infectious disease. In *Wikipedia*. Retrieved November 12, 2010 from http://en.wikipedia.org/wiki/Infectious_disease.

[2] Thunderstorm. In *Wikipedia*. Retrieved November 12, 2010 from en.wikipedia.org/wiki/Thunderstorm.

[3] Meteorology. In *Wikipedia*. Retrieved November 12, 2010 from en.wikipedia.org/wiki/Outline_of_meteorology.

[4] Cloud. In *Wikipedia*. Retrieved November 12, 2010 from http://en.wikipedia.org/wiki/Clouds.

[5] U.S. Navy Seal. In *Wikipedia*. Retrieved November 12, 2010 from en.wikipedia.org/wiki/United_States_Navy_SEALs.

[6] Respiratory System. In *Wikipedia*. Retrieved November 12, 2010 from en.wikipedia.org/wiki/Respiratory_system.

[7] Mythology. In *Wikipedia*. Retrieved November 12, 2010 from en.wikipedia.org/wiki/Mythology.

[8] Insect. In *Wikipedia*. Retrieved November 12, 2010 from en.wikipedia.org/wiki/Insect.

[9] Blood. In Wikipedia. Retrieved November 12, 2010 from http://en.wikipedia.org/wiki/Blood.

www.ingramcontent.com/pod-product-compliance
Lightning Source LLC
LaVergne TN
LVHW051602070426
835507LV00021B/2720